D1743381

NEURO-LINGUISTIC PROGRAMMING

10 NLP Strategies for a Fearless, Thriving, and Victorious Life – Build confidence, improve your social skills, develop effective communication, and reduce anxiety and stress

NEURO-LINGUISTIC PROGRAMMING

10 NLP Strategies for a Fearless, Thriving, and Victorious Life – Build confidence, improve your social skills, develop effective communication, and reduce anxiety and stress

TOM SHEPHERD

TABLE OF CONTENTS

INTRODUCTION

We don't know if that fall was rainier than usual at Bletchley Park in the UK. We don't know how the participants in what has been coined one of the largest cryptanalysis operations of the 20th century felt that morning. But we do know that, by the end of November 5, 1941, the Allies had in their hands one of the most powerful tools to help them sway the fate of the Second World War toward a victory for themselves. Led by Alan Turing, who would later become the father of modern computer science and machine learning, the team had finally broken Enigma, a tool the Germans had created to help them encrypt important strategic messages.

As you can imagine, this had the power to change the entire course of history. Alan Turing and his team at Bletchley Park wore no guns. They were not a part of the military. They weren't even computer scientists, as the field itself had not been invented yet.

They were, however, determined to crack the code. To make it happen. To break the inherently unbreakable messages from the Germans and bring at least a glimmer of hope for the Allies.

And oh, they did it! Not only did they crack Enigma, which was one of the most impressive pieces of war technology created by the Germans during that time. In this process, they managed to crack the dawn of a new era for the entire mankind, a dawn where computers and humans could finally communicate.

It took decades until the first personal computers entered every household. But many current analysts track the beginning of today's tech to what must have been a pretty chilly morning of November at Bletchley Park when Alan Turing *cracked the code*.

You see, communication can be a terribly influential thing. It can help you express your love for your life partner. And it can make or break wars.

Communication moves past words, though. Words are easy to toss around like there's no tomorrow. Real communication happens deep inside, in the "code" your brain is wired with, and only when the code has given its go-ahead will the communication be sent out to the "outside."

The best news is that you are not born with that code. And the even better news is that you don't have to live with a code you had no conscious, direct participation in building. You can actually reprogram your brain to communicate more efficiently and to be able to build bridges of communication between you and your innermost self, as well as between you and everyone else around you.

This is where we wheel in neuro-linguistic programming.

The book at hand is meant to be an introduction into the madly fascinating world of NLP—a practice that helps you rewire your thoughts and materialize them first into proper communication and, as a result of that, into successful actions.

Our book does not promise to make you rich, thin, or even remotely famous. It promises to make you *full*—to help you achieve your fullest potential and your biggest dreams and goals. If your goals are in any way related to appearing on the front cover of the *Wall Street Journal*, then so be it. Use NLP to get yourself there. If your goals are to be fitter, then so be it. Let NLP guide you there.

And if your goals are simply related to better family life, then so be it. Bring NLP into your daily practice and watch it work its magic.

Please take "magic" as a metaphor here, though. Neuro-linguistic programming is far from being *magical*. We're not selling you fairy dust, nor are we talking about empty words. What we *are* giving you is genuine information, the kind that can shift your life for the better in every way you can imagine.

In front of you lies a book that doesn't promise to take you to the moon (and back); instead, it promises you to help you find the most amazing tool Earth has ever seen: your own brain and the awe-inspiring force of change it can be.

We will start with a short introduction into how neuro-linguistic programming connects to the idea that your brain's main actions are tightly connected to software that both nature and circumstances have built for you. We will show you how two great minds of the twentieth century managed to crack a code in a way similar to what Alan Turing himself did, and how they then created a connection between the human brain, linguistic process-es, and behavior.

And once that brief intro is done, we will dive a little deeper into the main concepts that make NLP what it is: subjectivity, consciousness, and learning.

Have we stirred your interest?

There's more! There's so much more to neuro-linguistic programming that it would be virtually impossible to en-compass it all in *one* book. An encyclopedia? Maybe. But an entire three-story bookshelf would probably be more appropriate. And if you want to get really in-depth with neuro-linguistic programming, it would probably take an entire library.

Once we show you the very basic concepts behind NLP, we aim to teach you more about the principal steps you can (and should) take to embrace neuro-linguistic pro-gramming in your life. Look at these steps as the foundation of your new home, the very grounds upon which you will start building and solidifying your future neuro-linguistic programming practices.

We also aim to show you what neuro-linguistic programming is actually used for, both in terms of the fields of study it has touched and in terms of the day-to-day applications it can have. To effectively do this, we have included two short chapters that will detail the most common uses and applications of NLP.

Because neuro-linguistic programming is essentially connected to communication at its deepest level, it only makes sense that we have dedicated an entire chapter to elaborate on this specific connection as well. What's more, we will take a deep-dive into communication models from both the traditional perspective and from the perspective of NLP so that you can fully understand the way in which neuro-linguistic programming changes the entire paradigm.

Next, we will take a look at the actual programming language you can use to improve your communication skills. First, however, we will explain the three main ways in which human brains process information. It may not be surprising to you, but your brain processes a ton of information every second of your life (even when you are asleep!). So it naturally needs special techniques to filter out all this data and redirect it to the appropriate "buckets."

As you will see, this can be a major issue in communication, but we don't want to spoil this entire chapter for you, so we will leave you with that for now. We will use Chapter 7 to get more in-depth on how your brain functions and how it creates programming languages and methods to cope with all the information that bounces off of it every day.

Chapter 7 will also end the first part of this book, one which we have dedicated entirely to helping you understand the main *theoretical knowledge* behind neurolinguistic programming.

Chapter 8 will be all about the specific NLP strategies you can apply in your life and the exact techniques you can embrace to change your life and achieve fearlessness and victory on all of their levels. We have picked 10 strategies to help you with various areas of your life. Some of them are very easy (and they are very directly connected to the theoretical knowledge we will explain in the first part of the book too). Others are a bit more complex, and, to those of you who are still new to everything connected to self-development, they might sound downright odd. We promise, though, they all work.

Last, but definitely not least, we will dedicate the final chapter of this book to help you implement everything at your own pace. In many ways, this chapter will be a review of everything you have learned thus far, but not in the sense that it will reiterate the specific information you have read throughout the book. This will be a review meant to help you allow all the information to cement, to take root, and to flourish into a thriving life, the life you genuinely deserve.

Nothing can be scarier than change itself. As human beings who have settled into little villages and left hunting and gathering behind, we are quite reticent to change. The world around us has changed drastically, and, in the last 200 years, the speed of change has been tremendous too!

Despite all the changes we are all facing (some of which the much beloved, aforementioned Alan Turing actually jump-started), we are pretty odd when it comes to change. We are wired to not shift our ways very easily. Everything we are becomes a cemented building at some point in our lives, and unless we consciously bulldoze the negativity out of that building, we are bound to be left with it forever.

NLP is the shockwave you need to trigger change, and even more than that, it can be *the* change itself. It can be the one bell that will ring out in the dark, calling you to reach out and touch your dreams.

Because yes, making dreams come true is more than possible. And there are *so* many people who can attest to this that it would be redundant to even mention it. Goals happen. Happiness happens. Fulfillment happens.

But more often than not, they do not happen on their own. They take hard work to implant and grow in your mind and in your soul. They take sweat and yes, sometimes, they take a bunch of tears, too.

We hope the book at hand will help you plant that seed of happiness and grow it into the life you have always wanted to have. Because, just like every other human being on

Earth, you deserve nothing less than genuine joy and achievement!

You deserve to be your *fullest and most amazing you.* And, in our experience, neuro-linguistic programming can help you with that by tearing down the walls and allowing you to *create* a new, better version of yourself.

It's time to embrace You 2.0. The *you* that will make your dreams come true!

CHAPTER 1:
NEURO-LINGUISTIC PROGRAMMING:
THE SOFTWARE BEHIND YOU

Neuro-linguistic programming is not empty words that promise you the world and deliver nothing in exchange for your efforts. In fact, neuro-linguistic programming is as scientific as personal development can get.

Created in the 1970s by Richard Bandler and John Grinder in California, neuro-linguistic programming is a real, science-based approach to not only personal development but communication and psychotherapy in general as well.

According to the creators behind this approach, there is a strong connection between the brain's neurological processes, language, and behavior learned through experience. The three elements of this connection make up the name of the approach itself: neuro (for neurological processes), linguistic (for language) and programming (for behavioral patterns). When used together and in a controlled way, this approach can help people achieve different goals in life.

Basically, neuro-linguistic processing allows you to "copy" the skills exceptional people have and acquire them as your own. Not only does this help with self-development, but it can help with a series of issues, including depression, psychosomatic illnesses, phobias, learning disorders, and even a common cold.

Neuro-linguistic programming is frequently used by companies who want to train their teams in management. But maybe even more relevant for the purpose of this book is that neuro-linguistic programming has been used by thousands and thousands of people who managed to turn their lives around and engineer the experiences and the life they actually wanted, as opposed to letting chance, luck, and external factors move them around at their own will.

Early neuro-linguistic programming (NLP) was based on a methodology its creators called *modeling*. In addition to that, Bandler and Grinder also brought forward a set of techniques they created based on the first applications of their methodology. Bandler and Grinder only set the stage for an approach that was propagated through the decades and has been improved, re-shaped, and continuously used by a lot of people in the self-development field–including renowned therapist Virginia Satir and psychotherapist Fritz Perls.

The entire theory behind NLP starts with the idea that the human brain is somewhat of a computer, and therefore, it can be *codified* into doing things a specific way. In order to program your brain to achieve what you want to achieve, a specific language must be used. The *modeling* methodology was initially used on Virginia Satir to create what Bandler and Grinder called a *meta-model*–the ultimate model that allowed them to collect information and use it in challenging a client's way of thinking.

Once the programming language was acquired, the therapists were able to challenge the linguistic distortions and recover information that was deleted from their clients' statements. During those first sessions, concepts like surface structure, deep structure, anchoring, future pacing, and representational systems were born–concepts that continued to be used in the practice of neuro-linguistic programming.

Many have talked about neuro-linguistic programming, both as supporters and as detractors. But what remains, after all the storms and more than four decades after the beginning of NLP, is the long list of people that have used this approach and have succeeded.

By the late 1980s, neuro-linguistic programming was well out of the woods of the uncertainty. It had developed into a full-blown industry, one that was congruent with a larger movement, that of the *human potential*. Thousands of people fell in love with the practices covered by the human potential movement–and the more people fell in love with it, the more they were showing the world that, yes, it *does* work.

Neuro-linguistic programming makes sense from every single point of view. It makes sense because it is all based on how the human brain works. A computer built by nature, our brain is capable of computing information in ways not even the most advanced computers in the world now, in 2019, can.

Yes, we might be on our way to building artificial intelligence that can relate to emotions and process information just like the human brain does. But the truth is that we have a long way to go until that point.

What we have learned from computers, however, is that our brains are just as programmable as theirs are–and the power to "program" our thoughts and actions lies in our hands only.

Following, we will introduce you to some of the main concepts behind neuro-linguistic programming, as well as some of the techniques and sets of practices that make NLP what it is today.

The Main Concepts Behind NLP

The entire theory that moves the "wheels" behind the neuro-linguistic programming practice relies on one simple fact: Our brains are computers, and computers are (obviously!) programmable.

That makes sense, right?

When you read about the main components of neuro-linguistic programming, it will all make even more sense.

There are three main pillars supporting the NLP theory– three concepts that propagate the theory into practice and make it genuinely useful for those who participate in it.

The three main concepts are as follows:

1. Subjectivity. Nobody experiences the world objectively. No matter how objective you may try to be, you will always be subjective. You experience the world through your own prism, with your own pair of glasses. What might be a great perfume for you might not be as great for someone else. And your childhood experiences might not make sense or they might not affect someone else the same way as they do with you.

Humans create subjective representations of their experience – and they do so through their five senses and through language. Vision, olfaction, gustation, audition, and tactician help you perceive the world in a certain way. When you recall a memory, you will not recall just the objective information – if it's something that truly marked you in a way or another, you will most likely recall something related to the fragrance of that memory, the place, the colors, and so on.

According to the NLP theory, this kind of memorized experience has a specific structure, somewhat of a pattern that allows your mind to store out these experiences and describe them using a *natural* language.

Behavior itself can also be understood from the point of view of these subjective representations. In this understanding of behavior, verbal and non-verbal communication are included, as well as maladaptive and skillful behavior.

In NLP, all behavior can be modified (or re-programmed, if you want to put it that way) by manipulating the subjective representations mentioned above.

2. Consciousness. In neuro-linguistic programming, it is believed that there are two types of consciousness: the conscious one and the unconscious one. Subjective representations happen in the unconscious mind.

3. Learning. In neuro-linguistic programming, learning is based on *modeling,* or, in other words, imitation through codification and reproduction. One of the most important elements in the process of codification consists of the linguistic and sensory representation of the subjective experiences of the person who executes the expertise.

We will tackle these components in more detail throughout the following chapter; this was just an introduction to show you the absolute basics of NLP and how they make perfect sense.

Neuro-linguistic programming does not promise the impossible. It just promises a method by which you can actually rewire your brain to lead you into a better, more successful direction. It gives you the tools to access your inner software and reset it to a mindset that will *get you places* instead of making you spin around in circles.

Everything in nature is programmed to follow a very specific behavior, one that benefits the entire ecosystem. The sooner you understand this, the sooner you will also understand that you are part of the same programming system as well and, more importantly, that you can use your senses and your experiences to model yourself after *whoever* you want.

In the following chapter, we will discuss the main components behind neuro-linguistic programming in more detail. After that, we will dive into the applications of NLP, as well as how and in what ways NLP is tightly connected to communication.

Chapter 2:
The Main Steps to Neuro-Linguistic Programming

At its very core, NLP is quite simple: it is a method used by various types of therapists to rewire the human brain into thinking and acquiring specific habits, a specific mindset, or doing specific actions meant to help the person attain a goal.

According to the original creators of neuro-linguistic programming, Bandler and Grinder, in their book, *From Frogs to Princes*, a multitude of differences set NLP apart from other types of communication or psychotherapy practitioners. As the authors of the book put it, when they created this approach, everyone else was all about metaphors and theorizing. According to them, these types of metaphor didn't work—all they did was confuse people and not help them learn what they actually had to do to change their lives around.

NLP came as a response to all this. What Bandler and Grinder wanted was a method everyone can relate to and everyone can actually apply step-by-step. Beyond theories that simply *say* how humans should be and how they should act and beyond metaphors, the original creators of neuro-linguistic programming wanted something applicable, actionable, and easy for people to understand. What others before them had called theorizing, they called *modeling*, because, this time around, they were bringing forward not just theory, but theory *applied*.

Bandler and Grinder knew that real-life is not theory, but actual, day-to-day existence that pendulates between thought and action. So, they thought of connecting the two through therapies that would help patients connect their wishes with their thoughts (and the language they use), and, finally, with the materialization of these issues.

Instead of bringing forward just another religion or a theory sustained by researchers who did not practice psychotherapy per se (which was frequent at that time), the creators of NLP brought forward something a lot stronger. Something people could almost put their hands on, try, and apply to their lives.

Neuro-linguistic programming was not born out of theory. It was born out of practice. As the creators of the concept retell the story in the aforementioned book, when they started modeling people, they would first ask them what outcome they were aiming for when they made a certain maneuver (such as touching someone a certain way). Most of them had no idea, but even more, they would be reticent to finding the outcome they were actually aiming for.

Initially, the main method of observation employed by Bandler and Grinder was to pay attention to what people *did* rather than say, as they believed this is far more important than what people say and more revealing in terms of their real behavior. They were not interested in seeing what they called "real," but in what they called "useful." This helped them arrive at a modeling approach that created *useful* descriptions.

What Bandler and Grinder lay as the foundation of back then was just the beginning. From thereon, NLP has shaped and re-shaped itself to forms that are even closer to the postmodern world citizen than ever before.

There is no *one* recipe to neuro-linguistic programming, but several. When you bring them together, however, they all come down to a few simple steps (they are actually simple, we promise).

Following, we will introduce you to the main steps of neuro-linguistic programming. Each sub-chapter below will be dedicated to one of the main steps you should take to create a "program" for your mind and help yourself follow through with your plans.

Define and Redefine Success

In today's world, you would be very much tempted to believe that success is defined by the amount of money and material possessions you hold.

But if you look closer at TV stars and musicians who seem to have it all, you will soon realize just how many of them still feel miserable—even surrounded by all the adoration of their fans, even surrounded by expensive houses and cars, and even with all the critical acclaim one can possibly get.

Truth be told, models of success are far rarer than they may seem. Even more, they are more than frequently connected not to material possessions, but to qualities these people have acquired over time. Truly successful people are resilient, they are continuous learners (and frequently self-taught, at least to a certain degree), and they have managed to turn failures into success. These people did not have a linear ascension to fame and wealth; they stumbled and fell, they came back again, they reinvented themselves, and they managed to genuinely pull through all obstacles that came their way.

Think of the people who are generally considered to be successful. Think of Bill Gates, Warren Buffett, Steve Jobs, Freddie Mercury, Mahatma Gandhi, Arnold Schwarzenegger.

Each of them has a different story, sure. But if you look closer at their lives, you will soon realize that there was no direct path to success. They did not buy the key to fame and innovation. They learned how to make keys that suited their talents, their interests, their lives, and their experiences.

Before you proceed on the NLP path, it is of the utmost importance that you define your success according to models that are real. Remember, chasing fortune and glamor is not the way to do it—chasing passion, relentlessness, and making a real change, will, however, lead you *up there*, where the real stars of this world live.

Some of the success factors you should definitely take into consideration include the following:

- Successful people usually tend to follow some sort of plan or strategy
- They have an organized way of thinking
- They are resourceful and full of energy (sometimes, it seems that this energy is endless)
- They can communicate efficiently with peers, with the public, at every level.

Know Your Path to Success

There is no prescribed recipe when it comes to success—every person is different, and, as such, every road to success is different as well. However, if we had to split it into well-defined steps, they would be the following:

1. Set a clear outcome. One of the main flaws in thinking the original creators of NLP noticed in their patients was the fact that they did not think of the outcome of performing a certain action; they just did it.

   The minute you know what you are aiming for, you have a clear end-goal. You know what all your actions are leading to.

Let's say, for example, that you want to lose weight. Simply telling yourself that you want to do this might not suffice—you need a clear number to aim for. And you need to take action to reach that number as well. You will probably start working out more, eating healthier foods, drinking more water and green tea, and so on.

Let's take another example. Let's say you want a college degree. That degree won't actually happen unless you start taking action, and in order to do that, you need to know what college you want to attend, what courses you want to take, and so on.

Nothing in life is achieved without setting the goal or the outcome of your actions. Sometimes, you do this partially involuntarily (such as, for instance, when you get off your seat and go have a glass of water, the outcome of this being the fact that you will stop feeling thirsty).

For other goals, however, you must be a little more direct and involved, and you have to consciously make the decision to start taking action.

In fact, your goal should be quite specific, and it should have the following characteristics:

- It shouldn't be a "dream." The difference between dreamers and achievers is the first aim for vague ideas, while the latter aim for specific goals.

- It should be something that is within your control. For instance, if your goal is to win the lottery, you will find that this is completely out of your control and that you cannot actually achieve it through actionable steps.

- It should be positively expressed. Yes, language plays a crucial role in neuro-linguistic programming (no surprise here!). So, your goal should be formulated in a way that is very positive too. For instance, if you want to get yourself out of financial trouble, saying "I am in control of this and will have a good financial situation" is better than "I will not be made redundant at work."

- It should be realistic. You cannot set a direct goal for $1 million when your bank account shows $10. You can aim for $1,000, $100,000, and increase incrementally. But in order for NLP to function on you, you must make sure your goals are attainable—even if the larger, end-goal is still quite far away.

2. Start to take action. Setting a goal means nothing if you don't start doing something about it. Weight loss, a college degree, or even having a glass of water will simply not happen if you don't make one first step in the right direction.

    It is important to measure your actions and do exactly what you are supposed to do for the best outcome. Not all outcomes can be achieved in *one* action—some will need a series of conscious decisions and actions to become a reality.

    Without action, your outcome is mere theory, and if there's something both of the initial creators of NLP stood against, it's precisely that: a theory that does not materialize into palpable, doable actions.

3. Notice the effects of your action. Monitoring your progress is crucial regardless of what type of goals you may have set, so make sure you take a close look at the effects of your action(s).

You might notice that you are going in a good direction—in which case you are to be congratulated, of course!

You might also notice that you are off-track or that you receive negative feedback from your actions. It is important to acknowledge this, especially since a large part of doing neuro-linguistic programming is all about knowing how to sense different situations, how to interpret them correctly, and how to use the information you acquire this way to take further action.

4. Evaluate and re-strategize. Sometimes, we think the best course of action is something that is completely wrong (for various reasons). The best part about this is that you can use your mistakes and re-shape them into a new strategy. The more you know about what doesn't work, the more likely it is that you will find the best path to achieving your desired outcome.

When something goes wrong with your plan, don't give up. Don't despair. Don't think you cannot do it (because you *can*). Instead, take a step backward and think of the things that went wrong. Evaluate your position and re-formulate your plan. Create a new strategy that includes all the information you have collected from your mistakes.

The NLP Foundation

Neuro-linguistic programming is something you have to believe in—not necessarily in any kind of religious sense, but in the sense that you need to be in the right mindset to be able to reap all the benefits NLP has to offer.

You don't have to turn your whole world upside down to get the hang of NLP. You don't have to eat a certain way or live according to very specific habits and routines.

You have to work with who you are and what your main goal is. And, yes, you have to embrace the four pillars supporting the entire neuro-linguistic programming theory in itself:

1. Understand where your own mind map ends and where other people's maps begin. There's no

such thing as an objective point of view. Nobody can be 100% objective—not even a super-fast, super-smart AI (it will be biased to the biases of its programming too!).

Everything in the world is perceived subjectively. Where you see the green color a certain way, your sibling may see it slightly differently. Where you see a certain complex situation a certain way, your loved one may see it completely differently.

We see the world through the lens we have created for ourselves. Our personality, our character, our behaviors, our backgrounds, our education, and everything that has ever happened to us in the past create a certain point of view on everything else.

To fully embrace the NLP philosophy, you first and foremost have to understand where your own "mind map" ends and where other people's maps begin. In other words, you have to understand that your actions can only expand into other people's space for so long—after that, it's all up to them.

For example, if you have someone in your life who is an alcoholic, your mind map will want to expand into theirs to help them quit the habit. However, you have to understand that there is only so much you can do when it comes to other people's maps. Even more, you have to understand that your mind map affects *you* first and foremost.

2. Deep inside every behavior is a positive intention. This tends to be poorly understood and downright misunderstood in the sense that many people believe this is a naive way of seeing the world.

However, this pillar of NLP is *not* about believing that everyone is good in a moral sense. No, not everything people do is ethical.

However, at the base of every behavior, every person has a positive intention, something that will benefit them in one way or another. Nobody does things to harm themselves—not intentionally anyway, and even when we are discussing self-destructive behaviors, they still have an underlying positive intention (i.e. they might be a coping mechanism, for example).

3. Your communication's meaning will inevitably produce effects. The way you talk and the way you think are shaping your reality. As mentioned before, we're all subjective, and as such, the lens we use to view everything in life will naturally influence the way we perceive our life and the way it will shape up ahead of us.

For example, if you look at the clouded sky one day and think that *it's a pity it's going to rain*, your reality will be affected by it because you will see the upcoming shower of rain as a negative experience.

If you look and say, *oh, that's great, it's going to rain and agriculture will benefit from this*, you're already re-shaping your worldview and thinking in positive terms.

The "secret" Law of Attraction, another theory on how our thinking shapes reality, is very close to neuro-linguistic programming in this sense. What NLP does better, however, is to provide you with the actual *how-to* on how to use positive thinking to re-shape your present and your future.

4. Failure is a constructed concept—it does not exist. There's no such thing as failure, and this is something successful people understand *very* well. You may not win one battle, but not winning it will always provide you with a new perspective on what you are doing right and what you are doing wrong.

    Failure is subjective. Only *you* can actually perceive yourself as a failure, and as such, failure as a concept does not exist because it cannot expand beyond your own mind map. People perceive you as you project yourself to be, and if "failure" is how you define yourself, they will start believing in it. That is the only way failure "exists" is, thus, *in your head.*

5. Re-shape the way you understand "learning." At its very core, life is a learning experience. It doesn't even matter if you're religious, what religion you follow, or if you are completely agnostic

or even atheistic. Life is a journey of learning—and oh, my, what a beautiful one it can be when you set your mind the right way!

In neuro-linguistic programming, learning is perceived slightly differently than in other approaches. Basically, NLP says that your learning will move through four basic stages:

- Unconscious incompetence - you don't know and you don't know what you don't know
- Conscious incompetence - you realize there are things you don't know
- Conscious competence - you acquire the learning and become consciously competent
- Unconscious competence - you are an expert in your field, and you have reached a point where you do things well at an unconscious level without actually explaining how you do it.

Getting into NLP is, in itself, a learning experience. At this point, because you are reading this book, you are already in the second stage of learning according to the aforementioned schema. By the end of the book, when you will already start to apply the techniques we will describe, you will already be in the third stage of learning.

These are the mindset presumptions you should start with when proceeding on your journey to neuro-linguistic programming. You have to understand that only you can change your life, you have to understand that all behavior has underlying good intentions to it, and you have to understand that your communication (internal and external, with yourself and with everyone else) shapes your life. More than anything, you have to understand that failure is impossible; you may make mistakes, you may fall, and you may do it repeatedly. But that's not "failure." It's "feedback" you can use for your future attempts and your future learning.

NLP does not promise you the Moon overnight. It takes work to self-program your mind into thinking a certain way (a positive, constructive, successful way). But then again, Rome wasn't built in a day, and none of the successful people you have ever admired and followed have created their fame in the blink of an eye.

Yes, NLP takes work. But it also guarantees that your work will be repaid precisely because it works independently of everything and everyone else and you are the only one you have to rely on for this to work.

The following chapter will show you why it's worth giving neuro-linguistic programming a chance and why it actually works. After that, we will dive into the deeper applications of NLP and how they can help you materialize the entire theory behind this approach into actual actions and actual outcomes.

CHAPTER 3:
WHY NEURO-LINGUISTIC PROGRAMMING WORKS AND WHY LEARN IT

We're more than certain that you have heard about a million and one ways to make your life better. We won't give names here, for the simple reason that we're not trying to compare NLP with any of the other life-enhancing methods out there. In the end, what may work for some, may not work for others—and the other way around.

The thing with neuro-linguistic programming is that it's not just random mumbo jumbo trying to convince you that your life is in your hands.

We are more than certain that you know that already. You know very well that you are the only one who can take control of your life and shape it as you wish. Deep inside, we all know it, even those who might be more inclined to believe *destiny* is a premeditated affair.

NLP comes to show you *how* to turn your own brain and your own language into actual, real-life success.

And it works. It really, really does. As you will see in our next chapter, neuro-linguistic programming is not the kind of concept that applies to self-development only.

Going back to the topic of this specific chapter, though, you may wonder how is it that NLP works?

Well, as we were pointing out at the beginning of the book as well, neuro-linguistic programming works because it is based on a simple principle: Your communication projects your life.

There are countless pieces of evidence when it comes to the efficiency of NLP. The more haunting (and perhaps among the most persuasive) ones are those that tell the stories of those who have tried neuro-linguistic programming and have managed to see a change in their lives. The Association for NLP[1] has collected numerous such stories, from people who claim NLP has helped them with a wide range of issues, including (but not only) the following:

---

[1] NLP Case Studies - How Could NLP Help Me? - NLP - Neuro-Linguistic Programming. (2019). Retrieved 22 July 2019, from https://anlp.org/how-could-nlp-help-me.php

- Anxiety
- Creativity
- Confidence
- Dyslexia
- Acquiring better business skills
- Education
- Phobias
- Wellbeing
- Parenting
- Relationship

… And the list goes on and on and on.

Some of you might not be persuaded by stories from former users, and that could be understandable from at least one point of view. These stories are all, in the end, very subjective, so we can fully see why you might still be skeptical as to whether or not NLP is actually efficient.

At the same time, do keep in mind that there are literally hundreds of stories that all claim the same results: Neuro-linguistic programming has helped these people re-shape their lives according to their own wishes.

There are even studies that have been run in this direction and proven that NLP can, indeed, help people overcome certain situations.

For instance, in a study conducted by S. Ashok and S.R. Santhakumar, *NLP to Promote TQM for Effective Implementation of ISO 9000,*[2] in 2002, the authors proved not only that neuro-linguistic programming works at a personal level but that it can actually be applied to project management as well.

Their assumption was that even after the implementation of a quality standard like ISO 9000, team members would not be keen on maintaining the same level of quality, as they are not personally invested in the success of what they do. As a result, the authors of the aforementioned study said that techniques such as *kaizen* (a concept borrowed from Japanese Agile Project Management and Kanban) can be connected to NLP for better efficiency.

---

[2] Ashok, S., & Santhakumar, A. (2002). NLP to promote TQM for effective implementation of ISO 9000. *Managerial Auditing Journal,* 5(17), 261-265.

After running the study, the authors came to two main conclusions:

- Neuro-linguistic programming can actually enhance the activity of low performers in the team
- NLP helped the team improve their motivation, as well as their level of creativity

In other words, they proved that there is a tight connection between neuro-linguistic programming and the efficiency of their teams' *kaizen*.

Perhaps not surprisingly, this is not the only research that has been run in the same direction to prove the efficiency of neuro-linguistic programming.

Needless to say, these papers have really managed to show, time and again, that NLP is not a new-age ramble. It is just as real as any element of the behavioral studies, and it can show tremendous success in multiple types of cases.

We will not dwell too much on this—not because there aren't pages and pages that support neuro-linguistic programming, but because we want to keep everything on the positive side.

And if you are not fully convinced, just stop and think for a moment:

1. Why would something false survive for so many decades now?
2. Why would anyone lie about the efficiency of NLP?
3. Ultimately, what do you *really* have to lose by trying it?

We are quite sure the answers you give to the aforementioned questions will be the ones to convince you as well.

As mentioned before, believing in NLP is extremely important. So, take your time to sort this out with yourself before jumping head-first into the following chapters. As we progress with this book, our advice will get closer and closer to and farther from *why*. So take your time at this stage and come to terms with everything we have brought forward so far.

It will help going forward!

CHAPTER 4:
WHAT IS NLP USED FOR?

Most of the time, people associate neuro-linguistic programming with self-development.

And that is not completely incorrect.

NLP can absolutely help you become the best version of yourself. This is what the book at hand is all about in the end.

But you should also know about the multiple applications neuro-linguistic programming has—beyond the ever-expanding borders of self-development, beyond the limits of those who are still skeptical about it.

Therapy

It is perhaps not surprising to anyone, but NLP is used in therapy. Originally conceived with psychotherapists as models, neuro-linguistic programming has been acknowledged to influence a variety of modern-day practices, like the solution-focused brief therapy, for example. The main bridge of connection between NLP and modern psycho-therapy lies in its refraining techniques, which aim to help patients achieve behavioral change through a change in the context or meaning.

There are two main therapeutic uses for neuro-linguistic programming:

- It can be used by therapists as an adjunct to other therapies
- It can be used as a specific therapy (which is referred to as neuro-linguistic psychotherapy)

In both cases, NLP as therapy is fully acknowledged by medical and specialty bodies, and in some countries (such as the UK, for example), it is fully accredited by the official government organizations as well.

Alternative Medicine

Unfortunately, alternative medicine is both poorly understood and at times downright misunderstood. Practices such as acupuncture, aromatherapy, and Ayurvedic medicine have been used to help with certain ailments for thousands of years—and successfully so.

And yet, even with all the testimonials, people are still skeptical about it as "official" medicine, and science has made little to no effort in trying to prove the veracity of such practices.

In its incipient stages, neuro-linguistic programming too promised to cure a wide range of both physical and mental conditions, including dyslexia, epilepsy, and myopia. We will err on the safe side here and say that no conclusive evidence has been brought to support these claims.

We wish this book to be a comprehensive view of what neuro-linguistic programming is and how it can be used to make your life better on a variety of plans. At the same time, we advise you to consult with your physician or medical practitioner too. While NLP can help with physical and mental ailments, the purpose of this book is not to expand on that topic.

This is not to say NLP doesn't work for specific medical conditions. Au contraire! However, when it comes to serious medical problems, neuro-linguistic programming should, perhaps, be used as a support system, rather than the main therapy.

What can be said for certain is that, in the plan of self-development and psychotherapy, neuro-linguistic programming is a valid practice. As mentioned before, it is actually acknowledged by medical bodies and used as a stand-alone practice or as an adjuvant.

CHAPTER 5:
NLP APPLICATIONS

As you have read in the previous chapter, NLP can be expanded into a multitude of fields (and we have only scratched the surface with what we described!). Beyond the theoretical expansion of neuro-linguistic programming, though, there is an even vaster and more intriguing range of actual applications in which NLP can work its wonders:

1. Persuasion. There are several approaches to persuasion, but at the end of the day, you cannot be a persuasive person if you don't believe in yourself. NLP can change that context for you, and it can help you become more persuasive as a result.

2. Sales. Persuasion and sales are very tightly connected, so it makes all the sense in the world that those who want to improve their sales skills would benefit from NLP the same as those who want to improve their persuasion skills

3. Management training. Neuro-linguistic programming can alter your mindset, and in many

situations, that is the best place to start with when it comes to management training. So, again, it makes a lot of sense that NLP has been successfully used in management training as well.

4. Sports and fitness. Now, NLP can't get you out of bed at 5 am for a two-hour jog, but what it can do is alter the way you perceive this. Because it works with your mind (and thus, with the primary "control unit" of your body), neuro-linguistic programming can help you achieve better fitness and sports performance.

5. Team building. There are a variety of NLP techniques that can be used in team-building to "reprogram" the way a team works (and, probably more relevant, the way a team *succeeds*).

6. Public speaking. Since neuro-linguistic programming is all about communication and rewiring your brain to communicate a certain way, it also makes sense that public speaking would be one of the fields that will benefit from neuro-linguistic programming.

This lists only six of the most common applications NLP has, even when you don't consider physical and mental illness ailment. There are far more applications to neuro-linguistic programming, and they have all been used for quite some time now.

Applied in your life, NLP can help you:

- Upgrade yourself to a better "version"
- Establish, maintain, and manage better relation-ships, both at a personal and at a professional level
- Become a better negotiator
- Sell better and more
- Create presentations that entice and persuade
- Achieve better time management
- Be fitter and healthier
- Get the dream job

… And the list could go on and on, endlessly. Basically, whatever personal or professional goal you may be working toward right now can be enhanced by the use of neuro-linguistic programming.

How It All Works

Needless to say, neuro-linguistic programming is not rocket science. You can use it on your own self and see the results—and there is literally nothing to lose, but everything to gain.

We have already established that NLP starts from the basic presumption according to which the mind of a human being creates the "map" in which they live. In other words, what you think is what you get, and neuro-linguistic programming comes to help you rewire your thinking into success.

A "classic" NLP process takes into consideration six logical levels of learning and behavior, ordered according to their importance as such:

- Purpose and spirituality. This is all about things that are larger than *you*, and, perhaps, in a manner of speaking, larger than life itself. It might be about religion for some. For others, it might be about a spiritual system. And for others, it might be all about ethics. This is the highest at which one can change.

- Identity. This is all about how you perceive yourself, as well as how you perceive the role you play in your own life.

- Beliefs and values. This is the personal belief system everyone has, whether they are religious or not, whether they are spiritual or not. We all have a personal set of beliefs, and in NLP, this is a logical level that one can (and should) work with.

- Skills and capabilities. This is simple: It's the logical level of what you can do, the skills you possess, and so on.

- Behaviors. This is represented by the actual actions you perform on an everyday basis.

- The environment. This is represented by everything and everyone surrounding you: the context, the setting, the people around you. In neurolinguistic programming, this is the lowest level of change.

A typical NLP session in its more traditional stages would involve establishing a rapport between the patient and the therapist, followed by collecting information about the problems the patient is facing and their goal, applying certain tools and techniques to make any kind of intervention, as well as integrating a series of proposed changes.

The first stage was achieved by leading the verbal and non-verbal behavior of the client using specific techniques. Once the rapport was established, the therapist gathered information using a series of questions (frequently referred to as the "meta-model questions"). During this stage, the therapist/practitioner paid a lot of attention to both the verbal and the non-verbal responses of the client and encouraged them to think of the consequences of the desired outcome, as well as how their current behavior is influencing that.

The therapist might have also asked the client to visualize the results of actions that are more coordinated with their desired outcome. For instance, if the desired outcome is weight loss, the practitioner would have asked the client to visualize themselves eating healthy and working out and visualizing the actual results of that: how it feels to be thinner, how the jeans feel on them, the kind of sensations they experience, and so on.

Starting from there, the therapist began to re-shape the "map" of the patient, helping them create a bridge of communication between themselves, their goals, and their actions.

We know this might not sound very concrete, but bear with us. The next chapter is dedicated to explaining the connection between neuro-linguistic programming and communication itself. Although highly theoretical, this chapter will help you understand how, more exactly, NLP connects with communication, and how they both connect to actual, real-life behavior.

Following the next chapter, we will dive into the "programming language" behind neuro-linguistic programming and everything it entails. And last, but definitely not least, we will analyze ten of the most common NLP strategies you can use for a victorious life.

CHAPTER 6:
NLP AND COMMUNICATION

Communication is fundamental to human development.

It has been proven that some animals communicate with their peers as well, but when it comes to human development, communication lies at the very core of evolution itself. Without communication, we wouldn't have passed down everything we have learned in our incipient stages on Earth. And we wouldn't have been able to relay experiences that are fundamentally human: emotions, feelings, sensations.

In neuro-linguistic programming, it is believed that great communicators are characterized by:

- Their ability to know precisely the outcome of their communication
- A high level of sensory acuity
- Behavioral flexibility

All of these characteristics help good communicators establish better relationships.

What does that have to do with success and neuro-linguistic programming, you might ask?

Well, at its very foundation, communication is the core of every type of human relationship. And human relationships lie at the core of any kind of success you can imagine. Following the examples we have given in the previous chapter on how NLP can help you achieve certain goals, here's how communication connects into those goals:

- Persuasion is all about the relationship you establish with the person in front of you (or *group* of persons). Therefore, NLP can help you with this.

- Getting your dream job is all about acing the interview. And acing the interview is all about the relationship you create with your interviewers. Therefore, NLP can help you with this.

- Being fit and healthy is all about having a good relationship with yourself and your body. Once you can "communicate" with your body effectively, you can ace any kind of fitness goal you set for yourself.

According to Merriam-Webster, communication is defined as the exchange of information between individuals using a specific language, set of symbols, or behavior. [3]

We will dare to expand a little on this definition and say that communication does not always relay information in the purest sense of the word. Sometimes, it helps you relay emotions or sensations, for example. Moreover, communication does not happen between two individuals only; it can happen between one individual and a group of individuals as well (such as when you give a presentation in front of your board of directors, for example).

If you take a closer look at your own situation, you might realize that every single problem you might have is connected to a bad relationship you have with yourself, with a situation, with an individual, or a group of people.

Chances are that you wouldn't rate the quality of your communication in this relationship very highly, especially not when you look through the prism of the aforementioned characteristics.

---

[3] Definition of COMMUNICATION. (2019). Retrieved 15 July 2019, from https://www.merriam-webster.com/dictionary/communication

To help you understand just how important communication is in your life, imagine yourself as an excellent communicator—both when it comes to yourself and when it comes to others. How would your life look like if you were able to eloquently and elegantly express the information you mean to communicate with everyone in your life, including yourself?

Don't rush through this; it is an important step in becoming conscious of just how crucial communication has always been in your life (and just how much you may have neglected it, considering it an adjacent *tool* rather than a fundamental instrument in the making of your success).

Let's look at some examples.

If you are a salesperson (or want to become one), the way you communicate can make or break a deal. Imagine yourself being able to clearly convey the meaning of your thoughts to your potential customers. Imagine yourself being able to persuade them that your product is truly the best they can get, at the best price. Doesn't that look like success?

If you want to lose weight, you might not be able to communicate with yourself properly. Constantly telling yourself that you will start running and eating more salads on Monday is *not* proper communication. It is a mere "order" you want to give your body—but alas, your body doesn't listen to actual orders. Your body responds to proper communication, the kind that adjusts according to its behavior, to its responses, to what it wants, and what it truly needs.

If you have problems in your relationship with your loved one, communication may also be the main fault. Couples who stop communicating meaningfully stop connecting to each other, and when the bridge is broken, they might feel that they don't have much in common anymore. Days, weeks, months, and years can go by before one of the participants in a couple realizes they have no room in that relationship anymore; they have stopped communicating with their loved one and, as such, disruption has occurred. If, however, you were able to mend the bridge and re-connect, your relationship would naturally fall back on the right track again.

A life in which you are a good communicator is a life where you can create and maintain a healthy rapport with yourself and those around you. And as you imagine yourself in this life, you will soon realize that your interactions are fluid, your intonations come naturally, and the actions yielded by your messages are fully connected to the goals you have in mind.

Here's something that might blow your mind: The vast majority of the successful people you might follow and adore are, at their foundation, great communicators. Think of Arnold Schwarzenegger, for example. A bodybuilder by formation, Arnold knew how to communicate with his own self and push the boundaries of his body to win the competitions he was aiming for. Then, when he stepped into his acting role, he knew how to communicate with Hollywood representatives to let him play the role of Terminator (the one that rocketed him to success). Finally, as a politician, Arnold knew how to speak to the people he was meaning to represent.

Everything successful people like Arnold do and say sounds and looks right. It doesn't seem out of place, and that is because they are excellent communicators at their very foundation. Before being talented and hard-working sportsmen, before developing the acting skills that made them famous, before persuading the entire world to buy their products, before making the people believe in them and their ability to lead, all these people were great communicators.

Arnold Schwarzenegger is one example. Bill Gates, Steve Jobs, Warren Buffett, Mark Zuckerberg, and Elon Musk are others. And there are thousands of such models you can look up to every day. Instead of simply admiring them from afar, however, you can actually follow their patterns of success by acquiring the basic communication skills they have.

Take another moment and imagine yourself possessing these communication skills. Picture the life you would paint for yourself with these skills. Add whatever you want to make it complete and utterly happy.

In this picture-perfect scenario, how do people communicate back to you, verbally and non-verbally? How does it feel when you "hear" people talk to you like this? How does their body language change when they talk to you? Whatever it is, know that this is the result of the communication you have started with them, not the other way around.

Believe it or not, that image is within your reach. You paint it with your communication. Nobody else can do it for you, but you *can*.

Neuro-linguistic programming is all about that, about communicating properly. The initial work of Bandler and Grinder was based on modeling the strategies of fantastic communicators and hand-picking the elements that made a difference between them and those less successful than them.

For Bandler and Grinder, however, communication went past traditional message-sending and became an in-depth exploration of what happens to people's internal processes when they are communicating with other people. For Bandler and Grinder, communication went beyond the basic schema everyone knows; it expanded into the very structure of subjective experience.

This is precisely what sets NLP apart from other methods of self-improvement. It doesn't give you empty words, and it doesn't give you a set one-size-fits-all recipe for success either. It works precisely with who you are and the behaviors your communication elicits.

Communication Models: Traditional vs. NLP

The traditional communication model or schema involves the following elements:

- The emittent - the person who sends a message
- The channel - the actual channel through which the message is sent (air, phone line, internet, books, etc.)
- The code - the language (verbal or non-verbal) through which the message is sent
- The receiver - the person who receives the message

Depending on who was discussing this model of communication, other elements might have popped into the discussion as well, such as interferences, for example (e.g., noise that prevents you from being heard properly).

Beyond the differences that are more connected to the school of thought that they pertain to than anything else, all communication used to be encapsulated within the boundaries of the aforementioned elements. Whether we are talking about the communication between two individuals or the communication between an individual and a mass of people, everything humans ever wanted to relay was connected to these elements.

And for the most part, there is absolutely nothing wrong with the traditional model of communication. It is logical, it makes sense, it works.

What the traditional model of communication lacks, however, is an introspection into what happens internally when you communicate with yourself and others. This is where neuro-linguistic programming comes to fill in the gap and help you move past the traditional model.

The NLP model of communication takes into consideration the filters everyone applies when they come in contact with another person—the same filters that help your internal "mechanisms" create a certain type of "map."

In other words, the neuro-linguistic programming model of communication takes into consideration not only external interferences (like the noise in a crowded train station) but also the internal interferences like the way our own selves intervene with our communications and the obstacles we face when we want to communicate with ourselves and with others.

A successful communicator knows how to work with this map of obstacles. This person knows how to read and listen to this map in a way that helps them eliminate potential communication risks and mishaps. When you know how to work with the map your own "system" is building, you win the game, precisely because you know where your main strong points are, and you know where your less strong points are as well.

Most of the people create these maps unconsciously. Great communicators, however, know exactly where to "go" on their maps and how to work with what they have to get the very best results. The more conscious you become of your own map, the easier it will be for you to "rig" it and, eventually, to get to a point where unconscious competence dominates your communication.

To fully understand the NLP model of communication, you must first accept and acknowledge the fact that every single person on Earth is experiencing a constant ongoing stream of information. We are basically bombarded with information from the very first second we open our eyes in the morning to the second we go back to sleep. This is nothing *new* and it has nothing to do with the heavily digitized life we all live.

Our entire body is programmed to store all this information in different ways, in different storage units. To know exactly where each piece of information goes, our brains filter all the information using different techniques. Every person has their unique filters; there are no two people who apply the exact same set of filters and filtering techniques. These systems have been created over the course of the years since birth, and their specifics are influenced by our upbringing, our experiences, the people in our lives, and so on.

Our internal filters have three main purposes: to generalize (e.g., stereotypes are a way of generalizing information), to delete (e.g., you don't actually need to know what color the shirt of your bus driver was this morning), or to distort (e.g., when you are biased toward a certain person, you will distort what they do or say and fit it into a particular "box").

Our internal filters are also categorized according to their level of consciousness. For example, our language patterns are considered to be a conscious filter, precisely because it shapes our entire experience of reality.

In general, it can be said that your attitude in life is a filter in itself. Many times, we see the glass half empty or half full precisely because we have a pre-applied filter on everything that happens to us. Even more, our past experiences and memories can be filtered into a certain attitude toward life as well.

At the more unconscious level, you will find your value and belief system. Sometimes, they will activate at appropriate moments; other times, they might activate at inappropriate moments. Every time they do activate, however, they lead you to make judgments on what you can and cannot tolerate.

According to NLP, the most unconscious level of filtering includes what is referred to as "metaprograms"—habits and patterns that make us act the way we do for very specific reasons. These metaprograms are hard-wired into who we are and what we do in a way that is fully unconscious. Most of the time, you don't even question the *why* behind them. As a good communicator, however, you are able to recognize these metaprograms and use them to make better decisions and communicate better.

Let's bring all this theory into a concrete, real-life example.

Let's say you were bullied as a kid. Two decades after graduating high school, you meet your bully face-to-face for the first time since your days in school. Your internal filters will automatically associate this person with everything bad you have ever experienced with them. As a result, the image of them standing in front of you will correlate internally with a negative representation.

In its own turn, this negative representation will most likely connect to your lead sensory systems: visual, auditory, olfactory, kinesthetic, or gustatory. You might feel nauseous as if you ate something bad. Or you might associate this representation with a bitter taste in your mouth. This is your brain applying all the filters you have built for the person in front of you.

Good communicators know how to move past this and switch their representational systems. For instance, instead of feeling bad when they meet their bullies for the first time in decades, good communicators will switch to a positive representational system and they will see a grown-up who has made mistakes, perhaps a grown-up that is less successful than they are, or simply they will see themselves as grown-ups who have moved past the pain of their childhood bullying.

If you want neuro-linguistic programming to make a genuine difference for you, you must first understand the signals upon which your representational systems act. Once you understand those signals, you control them, and you can reverse-engineer the reaction you get to certain people or situations and re-shape them into something positive.

In many ways, it can be said that NLP is an art of change, adaptability, and flexibility. Instead of remaining rooted in your own biases, in the filters your brain has created for you, you will be able to move past those borders and recreate your own reality using a different language of representation.

In doing this, you will become a better communicator, both when it comes to those around you and when it comes to your own self. You will become more successful at what you do, you will be able to control your emotions and instinctive reactions better, and you will be able to grow more focused on achieving your goal, regardless of whether that is making your first million dollars or achieving better fitness.

CHAPTER 7:
NLP AND THE PROGRAMMING
LANGUAGE BEHIND IT

Alright, now that we have laid the groundwork for our book, it is time to get more in-depth with what neuro-linguistic programming actually looks like in its intrica-cies and just what a great role language itself plays in this self-development paradigm.

Let's start with how you perceive communication.

When you talk to someone, how much of the communi-cation do you feel responsible for?

Most people would think 50%, and it makes sense, since it takes two to participate in a conversation, right?

Well, according to neuro-linguistic programming, you are 100% responsible for the conversation—and so is your interlocutor as well. The meaning of your communi-cation and the response it triggers, whether or not what you are doing is working—these things are all in your power. The more flexible you are, the more you influence the system of communication created between you and your interlocutor.

Taking responsibility for every communication you emit is the first and most important step in acknowledging its very power. There are, of course, certain tools you can use in order for this to happen, tools that will help you understand your interlocutors and how *they* understand the messages they receive from you, how their thinking processes work, and how to adapt your own communication to achieve the response you want.

In our previous chapter, we discussed filters and how they affect pretty much every communication you receive.

The same filters affect your interlocutors as well. The behavior you elicit from your interlocutor is triggered by a chain reaction caused by your communication (an internal response). In turn, the person(s) in front of you will respond in a certain way (the external behavior). You will then react in a certain way as well, and a new chain reaction will be triggered in the person(s) in front of you.

That's how communication works.

When an internal response is formed, there are two main components that participate in it:

- The internal process (consisting of mental images and sounds, self-talk, and so on)
- The internal state (the feelings and emotions you are experiencing at the given time of communication)

When you are flexible and capable of controlling the aforementioned components of your internal response, you can control the outcome of your communication.

Let's look at two examples, side by side, of how a situation can play out if you allow your internal response to take its natural course and if you control your internal response.

You spent the whole night working on a report for your boss, a report you couldn't have possibly finished in the time you were allotted to finish it at work. You went to sleep at 5 am, aiming to wake up at 7 am and go to work. Instead, you woke up to the sound of your fourth alarm, at 8 am, and jumped out of bed.

Normally, you take the subway to your workplace, but now that you're in a hurry, you call for an Uber. There is a surge in orders, so you end up paying three times the normal price, wait four times longer, and have to sit through a never-ending trip to work as a bonus.

You get to work already very tired and irritated and assume that your boss will admonish you for being late. Before he even opens his mouth to say something, you instantly explode and tell him that your assignment was given too little time. This makes you look bad in his eyes because it sounds like you are putting the blame on him and you are trying to remove all blame from you. As a result, he gets angry and the situation escalates to a point where he storms out of the office threatening that this is your last day at your job.

Now, this whole situation could have been a lot different if you simply understood the communication processes behind your actions and behind the actions of your boss. If you would have gotten to work and waited for your boss to actually communicate with you, then apologized and explained the situation calmly, it wouldn't have escalated into a disaster. What's more, your boss would have understood how much work you put into the report.

So, How Do You Understand the Communication Process?

As mentioned before, there are three main characteristics great communicators have in common: They know what they want, they know how to notice responses, and they are flexible enough to change their behavior according to the aforementioned responses so that they can get what they want.

In order for all this to happen, you basically have to distance yourself from your own emotions and filters. If you focus on the result you want, rather than on all the filters "happening" in your mind at the time of communication, you will end up with far better results in terms of achieving the goal of your communication.

Of course, understanding your own filters and biases is not enough. You have to understand how the brain works at a very general level, or, in other words, you have to understand how *your* brain works and how other people's brains work as well.

First of all, you will have to understand that every second of your life you—and everyone else—is hit by millions of bits of information. You are most likely not fully conscious of just how much information your brain is processing, and that is precisely because of all the "filters" your brain activates to cope with this information.

Leaving out all the information your brain deems either unnecessary or automatic (such as colors and sounds for example), you can only process about seven bits of information at a time, according to George Miller's Information Theory.[4] Sometimes, you can process five bits, while other times you can process nine bits depending on your mood, on your interest in the current communication, and other similar factors. When you are completely uninterested, you can even process as low as one bit of information at a time.

Processing these bits of information is tightly related to the aforementioned actions the brain takes: deletion, distortion, and generalization. Let's take a closer look at how each of these actions functions and what they do; doing

---

[4] Information Processing Theory (G. Miller) - InstructionalDesign.org. (2019). Retrieved 22 July 2019, from https://www.instructionaldesign.org/theories/information-processing/

so will help you understand how the human brain works so that you can control your internal processes.

Deletion

When you selectively pay attention to the information coming toward you, the brain applies an action called deletion. In this case, you will pay attention to some of the information, but you will completely omit any other stimuli.

Think of a time when you were so stressed at work that you forgot to actually eat. Or maybe there was a time when you slept so poorly and in such a small quantity that you nearly left home wearing your pajama pants. When these things happen, it means your brain has used deletion. Of course, these might seem like very extreme examples, but the point of them is to show you that your brain proceeds to delete information all the time.

Distortion

Distortions are very closely connected to how humans attach their emotions and biases to the communications they come along with. Many times, deletion is associated with distortion as well.

For instance, if your relationship with your loved one has fallen apart, you might be tempted to only see the things they are doing wrong and associate those with everything else they do. In these cases, your brain would distort any information coming from the other person and overlap it with your own already-shaped viewpoint.

In most cases, xenophobia, antisemitism, and racism function the same way, with people shaping their own opinions about other people pertaining to a different nationality, ethnicity, or race, and then overlapping that opinion with everything their targets do.

Again, these are extreme examples, but just as with deletion, your brain resorts to distortion all the time. In most cases, this is a healthy thing to do because, as mentioned before, you simply cannot process all the information that comes at you on a daily basis. However, it is important to control your distortions and acknowledge when your system may have gone haywire.

Generalization

Somewhat similar to distortion, generalization is another common technique your brain uses to process information. For instance, if you gave a very good PowerPoint presentation once, you might think you are *generally* good at PowerPoint presentations. Sure, you might be, but you simply cannot base this kind of assumption on one occurrence only.

Just as with deletions and distortions, generalizations are actually useful because they help you create a cognitive map of the world you live in. If your brain couldn't generalize, you would have to learn a lot of things all over again—including the alphabet, how to spell words, how to do basic arithmetic, and so on. Imagine that!

At the same time, generalizations can be very limiting for your self-development. And the best example we can give here is that of how people who lack self-confidence will generalize their opinion of themselves and apply it to everything. If you constantly believe yourself to be *not enough*, chances are that you will constantly fail at what you aim for.

On the other hand, if you constantly believe yourself to be good at what you do, you will most likely achieve your goals on a constant basis as well. Of course, you might fail sometimes, but even when that happens, you will be able to move on with ease precisely because you won't take this to the heart.

Everyone deletes, distorts, and generalizes information. The trick is knowing that not everyone does it the same way. Each person builds a map of their own world according to their own mechanisms of deletion, distortions, and generalizations, and knowing how to recognize this pattern will eventually help you understand the way other people function and improve the way you communicate toward your desired goal.

Understanding the Mental Processes Behind Communication

You can't read people's minds, no matter how much you would like to.

What you can do, however, is to learn how people's brain "software" works. Or, more specifically, what is the programming that makes their brain apply the techniques we mentioned before: deletion, distortion, and generalization.

These metaprograms, as they are called by NLP specialists, are the filters people apply and which lead to certain behaviors. The interesting thing is that these filters are applied through language, which, if you think of it, is quite similar to how computer programs work.

Of course, computers don't speak English, Chinese, or sign language. They speak in different programming languages, like Pascal, C+, or Python. But these languages have their own set of rules, their own vocabulary, and their own way of functioning just like human means of communication have.

Your brain is not that much different than a normal computer; it is fair to say that, at least up to some extent, computers have been created in the spitting image of their creators, human beings.

People have learned to program computers, but sadly, to most of us out there, our own brains are an enigma in terms of programming. And that is precisely where neuro-linguistic programming fills in the gap, to help you program your own brain.

Circling back to metaprograms, knowing how to use these will help you achieve what you want from every communication, both when it comes to communicating with your own self and when it comes to communicating with others.

The language you use is a direct reflection of your metaprograms, and your metaprograms are a direct consequence of your language. The two concepts circle around each other, directly influencing each other as you go.

For instance, if you are a person who is generally proactive, you will be far more likely to say something like "I want to see the results, not the processes," while someone who is more reactive will most likely say "OK, but let's think of the processes behind this decision."

There are a lot of extreme tendencies people can lean toward, and these tendencies are, in fact, metaprograms. For example, introverted and extroverted behaviors are a mirror of two diametrically opposed metaprograms. Everything that an introvert does will be influenced by this metaprogram. And everything that an extrovert does will be influenced by this metaprogram as well.

Of course, most of the time, people are not 100% introverts or 100% extroverts; it is unlikely that you will ever meet someone who is either completely retreated in themselves or completely out in the open. However, the more you lean on one side, the more your metaprogram will lean toward behaviors associated with the more extreme tendencies.

Whether or not you lean toward one direction or the other depends on a lot of factors, including your education and upbringing, your own view of the world, your beliefs and values, as well as the precise context you are in.

For instance, you might be quite extroverted when you are among friends you have known for a while because you believe in friendship and because you feel comfortable around them. But when it comes to presenting a PowerPoint report in front of the entire board, you might not feel as comfortable, and as such, you might turn inward and lean more toward an introverted behavior.

Of all the factors that could influence your metaprograms, your values are among the most important. In the vast majority of cases, you won't be actually conscious of your values; they are seeded in you by your parents and close family up until the age of seven, and then by your peers and friends.

Your values should not be perceived as either negative or positive. Some of them help you move forward. But others, on the other hand, simply stall you (or even make you take steps back from your evolution). Your values have a pretty heavy influence on how your brain processes information through deletion, distortion, or generalization. Even more, how you hierarchize your values is, in itself, an influencing factor in how you process information.

Let's take a look at an example.

Let's say your value hierarchy looks something like this:

1. Being with your family
2. Being happy
3. Being able to make a change in the world
4. Being able to have variety in everything in life

If, for example, you were offered your dream job tomorrow, but it was on the other side of the world, you would probably either turn it down or communicate with your family and see how they feel about moving so far away.

Knowing what your values are is quite important when it comes to understanding your own self. To find out what truly matters for you, start by looking at an aspect of your life that is less successful than you might want it to be (your career, for example). Create a list of the things that matter to you when it comes to the aspect you have chosen. Take your time with this; if you feel the need, go through the list again and again, until you feel like you have nothing left to add in there.

Order the items on your list according to just how important they are for you. For instance, you might find that making a meaningful change is more important for you than working close to home or having a very large paycheck at the end of the month. That is perfectly fine— we each value our life's aspects differently.

Now, take each item on the list and think of what kind of deletion, distortion, or generalization you may be making about it that is preventing you from achieving your goal. Again, take your time and don't rush through this; it is very important to pay attention to each item on the list and be honest with yourself.

Last, but not least, take each item on the list and determine what are your limiting decisions, the ones that might impact your values.

Aside from your values, your beliefs can also influence your metaprograms. Although they might be easily mistaken with values, your beliefs are opinions you shape (rather than a hierarchy of meta-goals in your life). Some beliefs will be rooted in you since childhood—such as if your mother constantly tells you that you have a talent for music. Others will be acquired during the first years of school—such as when your math teacher tells you that you can't do much in life without math.

Your beliefs affect your mind and your outlook on life itself. If you believe you are good with music, you might feel confident enough to pursue a career in that area. But if your math teacher says math is the only way to build a better life for yourself, you might fall into this routine and choose a career based on engineering or programming, for example.

The good news is that you can change your beliefs; choose carefully, though, because once you have adopted them, they will shape your entire worldview.

The attitudes you have are also important in the way you shape your metaprogram. The way you think about a given topic, person, or group of people is all connected to your attitude.

Your attitude toward something specific is shaped by your values, your beliefs, and your opinions about that "something." Unlike with values and beliefs, however, attitudes are more conscious, and as a result, they might be challenging to change precisely because your mind is actively involved in holding on to them.

What people say and how they behave might reflect their attitude. For instance, if someone constantly rolls their eyes when they speak to you, it means that they have already formed an opinion on you, and their body language is reacting to that. What you could try is to have a very positive attitude toward a person like this (or a person with a negative attitude in general). You may be surprised, but positivity spreads like a virus!

The key point when it comes to attitude is that a *positive* one can actually change the outcome of your communication and actions. A negative one, however, will reflect on your actual behavior, and it will prevent you from achieving your goal.

Your memories also affect the way you build your metaprogram. Sometimes, you might not even be conscious of these memories, but they are in there, stored in your brain, influencing how you behave and anticipate communications with other people. Your memories affect you not just in the present, but they can affect your future as well.

When your brain accesses memories, it will instantly access the emotions it associates with the memories as well. As such, when you remember a nice day of playing around with your cousins, you will feel all those wonderful emotions. But when you remember someone dear who has passed away, the emotions associated with that sad event in your life will be accessed.

Your present experiences can access old memories you didn't even know of at a conscious level, and thus, they can access emotions associated with those memories as well. As a result, your present experiences will be filtered through your past memories, and this can alter the very way you communicate.

Decisions also affect your metaprograms. More often than not, the decisions you make are affected by the memories you have and, in their turn, will affect all the areas of your life. It is perfectly normal for things to be this way, but you have to be fully aware of the fact that some decisions might actually limit your options for the future.

For instance, if for your entire childhood you were told that you are not good at math, you may eventually make the decision of pursuing a career that is as far away from it as possible. In consequence, this will limit your options for the future—provided that you don't necessarily come back to study math.

And here's another example. If you grew up in a less financially stable environment and you one day make the decision that "once poor, always poor," this will obviously hinder your perspectives for the future.

Most of the limiting decisions are not made at a conscious level. Some of them are made when you are quite young. Others are made and then forgotten or left in an unconscious area of your brain.

Let's do a short recap of what we have discussed in this section. At its beginning, we were saying that your brain processes are affected by what NLP specialists call "metaprograms," which are software programs that have been embedded in the way your brain functions. These metaprograms can be influenced by a variety of factors, but the most important ones (which we have discussed throughout this chapter as well) include the following:

- Tendencies (extroverted and introverted)
- Values
- Beliefs
- Attitudes
- Memories
- Limiting decisions

When you become conscious of these factors, you can master the metaprogram instead of allowing it to run you from the "shadows" of your brain. If you know that, for example, your values are limiting your ability to reach your goals or that you have been displaying a negative attitude toward something, you also know how to fix that issue. And, as such, you can reprogram your brain to think differently—to think in terms of winning, and not in terms of limiting your own perspective on life.

Effective communicators engage with their metaprograms in a conscious way. For example, they:

- Process before they communicate
- Treat everything with caution
- Know that, at the other end of the communication channel, they will find people like them, with their own pre-installed metaprograms.

When you can do all of the above, you are already a winner. You are a person capable of not only winning friends but influencing the outcome of your actions too. You are a person who is well on their way to achieving their goals, regardless of whether those goals are related to career success, family bliss, financial freedom, or weight loss and fitness.

Use Your Senses!

Fortunately, we have been gifted with the ability to feel the world around us through much more than just words. We have been gifted with senses that help us move past the words and feel the way in which the world and other people are trying to communicate with us.

Until now, you have been introduced to the very basic tenants of neuro-linguistic programming: the communication process as seen by NLP specialists, the techniques our brain applies to process information, and the mental processes that lead to the creation of a metaprogram.

Sensory awareness (as it is called in NLP) is another crucial component of efficient communication. When you are able to understand how people make meaning of their own world map and how they use their senses to do this, you can become a better, more efficient communicator, one whose goals are always accomplished.

When you are born, you are given the tools to learn about the world. These tools are your senses: your eyesight, your hearing, your taste buds, your nose, and, perhaps, what is most important, your ability to create a human, emotional connection with other people.

As you grow, your mental maps start to shape as well. You learn about the world around you in the best ways that work for you, through your senses. And, eventually, your brain uses your mental map to create the metaprograms that influence your communications.

In neuro-linguistic programming, you are encouraged to learn more about your own mental maps and understand how your senses play into their shaping. Understanding this will help you notice how your own perceptions are formed and how they tie into your ability to communicate with other people.

The main downfall associated with knowing the world through your senses is that you might, at some point, become conditioned. In other words, your learning system will become lazier because it will notice that you have grown to be good at certain things and it will keep using the same method again and again and again.

For instance, if, as a child, your talent in music is praised by your parents and/or teachers, you might be tempted to repeat the same "recipe." Sometimes, you might even be tempted to repeat the same kind of songs that brought you praise.

The same thing can happen with your senses as well. When you become good at using one thinking method, you will naturally focus more on that, rather than trying something new. This is why we sometimes look without seeing, eat without actually tasting, hear without actually listening, and so on. We're used to these processes, and we take them for granted.

If you stop to pay attention to what your senses are telling you, however, you are far more likely to understand not only how your own world map is built, but how other people's are as well. Consciously focusing on your senses and the extra-messages they are trying to send you can benefit everyone—both you and your interlocutor(s).

What's more, getting fine-tuned with your senses will help you from multiple points of view, not just that of the communication as seen through the neuro-linguistic programming point of view. When you can allow your senses to let you experience life more intensely, you are happier. Music is better. Colors give you joy. Food is more delicious. And you are able to actually *seize the moment* every single step of the way, instead of basking in negativity and a negative attitude toward life itself.

That is another story for another time, though. Let's take a closer look at how you can use your senses to gain a better understanding of the world around you.

In principle, there are five senses people use to experience the world: seeing, hearing, smelling, tasting, and touching. However, from the point of neuro-linguistic programming, you filter information in three main ways:

- Visually
- Auditorily
- Kinaesthetically

These senses are frequently referred to as VAK in NLP. While the first two might be crystal clear (some people like learning through pictures and visual stimuli, while others prefer the auditory ones), the third one might need a bit of explanation. The kinaesthetic dimension is related to your touching senses—but its meaning doesn't include just that, and it transcends into the emotions touching senses raise in you. In other words, the kinaesthetic dimension is all about how your body reacts to learning materials.

For instance, reading this book, you may be holding the tablet or eReader in a certain way. You may be lying down in a certain way and then getting up for the more interesting parts of the book. Your fingers will swipe on the screen and feel a certain way. Some people associate these sensations with learning, and it helps them remember information easier and faster. Other people, however, prefer the visual stimuli, or the auditory one. And that's fine; we're different, and that's a marvelous thing to think of. In the end, what is truly important is that you know what works for you.

On a day-to-day basis, your brain accesses the visual, auditory, and kinaesthetic senses every time it encounters stimuli, and it does so with all of them at once. However, in most cases, one of the senses dominates (because your brain finds it easier to cope with that, rather than the other ones).

In NLP, the main factor behind someone's choice of one type of stimulus or another is called a "resourceful state"—a state in which you feel open and curious about learning and you can access all the resources your brain offers to solve the problems you are facing. When you are in your resourceful state, you feel that you are doing what you are doing because you *choose to*, rather than because you *have to* or *need to*.

The resources you engage when learning can be internal (such as a natural inclination or a desire to learn) or external (such as motivation you get from other people). In neuro-linguistic programming, the channels through which humans represent information at an internal level are referred to as "representational systems" or "modalities." According to the three types of stimuli that NLP specialists have identified to have a greater importance in learning, you will then speak about visual, auditory, and kinaesthetic representational systems per modalities.

The specific characteristics of each of these representational systems are called "submodalities." For instance, for the visual representational system, you might have color or brightness as the main submodality. For the auditory representational system, you might consider the tone of voice as a submodality. And for the kinaesthetic representational system, you might consider the pressure as a submodality.

The words you use in internal or external communication to denote all the sensory experiences are referred to as "predicates" in NLP. Words like "feeling," "taste," or "picture" fall in this category. Do not mistake these for the grammatical notion of "predicate"—the NLP predicates can be any part of speech (they can be nouns, verbs, or adjectives).

Why are these predicates important? Because you can use them to build rapport through words, or, to put it differently, to reshape your own map of the world through the words you use.

How About the Interlocutor?

Alright, so you have now learned more about how your own brain works and how it shapes your reality.

What about other people? How do you know what they think and how their brain works so that you can communicate effectively with them?

Well, all human beings follow the same principles. They all build world maps in their heads. And they all use the VAK dimensions to do that.

Knowing what specific dimension works better on your interlocutor can help you relay your message better, in a way that actually reaches them.

In principle, you have to follow their language very closely. For instance, if someone says that they are more likely to make important decisions because it "looks right," they are most likely a visually-stimulated person. If they say that they make these decisions because they "sound better," it means that they might be more inclined to react to auditory stimuli. And if they say that something "feels right" or that they follow their "gut feelings," it means that they are more likely to react better to kinaesthetic stimuli.

There are tests you can run on yourself when it comes to determining which dimension works better in your case. But you might not be able to test every person you meet, in which case it is important for you to bring the conversation toward something that will indicate whether they are stimulated visually, auditorily, or kinaesthetically.

This can be extremely helpful. For instance, if you have determined that your boss is a person who is more stimulated by visual stimuli, you can create presentations that are highly visual and focus a lot on the design. If, however, they are more of an auditory person, you can create presentations that sound right.

Do keep in mind that you should not generalize and "segment" people into the three aforementioned dimensional groups. A person can be better stimulated by visual factors when at work, but the same person may be more auditory when they are off the office grounds. Apply these "tags" in specific contexts instead of generalizing and putting people in small "buckets;" human beings are far more complex than that!

As mentioned before, knowing the modalities, submodalities, and predicates people prefer can help you build rapport through words—a bridge of connection that will help your communication get across in a clearer, faster, more convincing way.

All great communication starts with excellent listening, and communication from the NLP viewpoint makes no exception from this rule. To be able to determine what type of language someone prefers, you first have to listen carefully to them. Being flexible enough, you will be able to adjust your own language and linguistic patterns to match those of your interlocutor(s).

For instance, people who are stimulated by visual modalities are more likely to be heard using words and expressions that include the following:

- Bright
- Illuminate
- Clear
- Color
- Focus
- Graphics
- Perspective
- Vision
- This looks like...
- We look after each other
- This makes me see the world in a new light
- A sight for sore eyes
- This appears to...
- Look, this...

People who are stimulated more by auditory modalities will, on the other hand, be more likely to use words and expressions that include the following:

- Argue
- Discuss
- Harmony
- Melody
- Resonate
- Sing
- Vocal
- Outspoken
- Question
- It sounds like…
- I heard it myself, from his/her own lips
- Word for word
- Clear as a bell
- Tuning into…
- Music to my ears
- This strikes a chord

Last, but not least, people who are more inclined to be stimulated by kinaesthetic modalities are also more likely to be heard saying words and expressions like:

- Cold
- Firm
- Movement
- Grasp
- Solid
- Weight
- Flow
- Bounce
- Exciting
- It feels like…
- Get to grips with
- Solid as a rock
- Driving the organization
- This is a pain in the neck
- Taking it one step at a time

Sometimes, people use words that pertain to the olfactory and gustatory realms as well, such as pungent, smoky, sweet, fragrant, juicy, and so on.

Of course, people don't use solely words related to their senses when they communicate; that would be absurd, given that we are not beings that are based on *just* our senses. These words are considered to be non-sensory in the NLP field. They are neutral words because they do not necessarily connect you, but they don't disconnect you from your interlocutors at the level of the modalities used in thinking.

There are also instances when communication is very logical and lacks any kind of sensory language. In NLP, this is called "digital processing." You will encounter this type of wording more frequently in legal, medical, and corporate communications, but don't be surprised if you encounter people who speak similarly in their day-to-day communication as well.

It is quite important to reach some sort of consensus in terms of the language you use with your interlocutors. You shouldn't use a highly sensory language if you had to deal with a very legal context where only the technicalities matter. And, likewise, you shouldn't use a digital processing language when talking to your best friend over a cup of coffee either.

Adjusting your language to the one spoken by your interlocutor is important because it will make it easier for you to connect to them. Sometimes, even if people share points of view that are very similar, the lack of a communication bridge can be fatal to their actual communications. And sometimes, translators might have to intervene between people who simply cannot get along. Believe it or not, some communication bridges are so broken that it's hard to repair them if neither of the interlocutors understands how sensory language functions and if they are simply not flexible enough to adjust their own linguistic patterns to those of their partner.

That being said, translations will probably not be necessary in your case if you finish this book. You already hold more information about the way NLP communication works than the vast majority of people out there, so all you have left to do is *grow* on this.

Do keep in mind, however, that it might be difficult for you to adjust to a new group of people if you are used to communicating with your own group. Say, for example, that you work in IT and you normally use the same kind of representational systems and modalities as your peers and management. If, for example, you had to give a talk to a group of people working in agriculture, you might find that there is a disruption between how *you* communicate and how your addressed group communicates. And since you are the one giving a talk, it would be your job to adjust your language to that of your target audience.

Furthermore, it is more than worth mentioning that the more passionate you are about your job (or the scope of your communication), the more likely it is that you will use sensory language to communicate. For instance, someone who is taking their job at its face value might use stiff, logical language. But someone who is actually passionate about their job (even if it's something generally perceived as "technical") might be far more likely to use sensory language patterns when they communicate.

As you can see, communication is not a simple act. Most people do it more or less unconsciously according to the metaprograms and patterns their brains have already established for them. But once you get in-depth on this, you will very quickly realize just how complex communication can be.

The great news is that pretty much everyone can develop and change their sensory representational systems. The single most important factor in whether you succeed at this or not lies in how you are able to tune in to the person sitting in front of you to listen to how they speak, to observe how they behave, and to match your own language and behavior to theirs in a way that will help you achieve the goal of your communication.

This is not mumbo-jumbo, as mentioned in the beginning. It's just how we are built to function. It's the way nature has created us, and there are very good reasons these systems are set in place. Playing with them, however, can give you an edge and help you achieve what you want faster (and easier, too!).

Beyond the Spoken Language

Human beings are considered to be the only living beings capable of articulate language. Other classes of animals (and, according to some, even beings in the botanical realm) use communication too, but it is not articulate.

What is perhaps even more fascinating about human communication is that we never rely *solely* on actual language to communicate. More often than not, our words (be them spoken or written) are accompanied by what is generally referred to as "body language."

Obviously, all body language is important in determining the true message behind someone's communication. But in neuro-linguistic programming, Bandler and Grinder placed a lot of emphasis on the eyes and how eye movements are connected to the modality they are using in communication. According to the original thinkers behind NLP, the way a person moves their eyes says a lot about the modality they are accessing, as follows:

- When the eyes are positioned in the top right side, the pattern is visually constructed and the brain is thinking of a new or constructed image (like a flying pink tiger, for example)

- When the eyes are positioned in the top left side, the pattern is visually remembered, and the brain is thinking of an image they have seen before (their mother when they were children, for example)

- If the eyes stare blankly ahead, a visual pattern is accessed and the brain might be thinking of an image that is either new or remembered (such as focusing on what is important in a presentation or communication)

- If the eyes are positioned in the center-right side, the pattern is auditorily constructed and the brain is processing new or constructed sounds (such as a new song in a genre they haven't listened to before)

- If the eyes are positioned in the center-left side, the pattern is auditorily remembered and the brain is processing a familiar sound (such as your spouse calling for you from another room).

- If the eyes are positioned in the bottom left, the pattern is auditory internal and your brain is processing a discussion you are having with yourself (such as when you think of what you should eat today at lunch)

- If the eyes are positioned in the bottom right side, the pattern is kinaesthetic and your brain is processing a feeling, an emotion, or a sense of touch (such as when you feel the temperature of your child's forehead with the back of your hand).

You can test out these observations as well. Take a friend and give them stimuli similar to those in the examples above and see what happens to their eye movements. For instance, if you tell them to picture a pink flying tiger, you might notice that their eyes move to the top right side as they try to imagine this.

Being able to determine the VAK dimensions you access and those that your interlocutors access can yield a lot of amazing results. Some examples include:

- Being able to influence the way a business presentation or meeting goes because you can actually connect to your audience and give them information in their own language
- Creating balance in your own family by assigning everyone the tasks they are more prone to like and by speaking to everyone in their own language
- Setting goals that are realistic and coordinate with how you use your senses
- Setting goals you can actually picture according to your preferred modality and submodalities
- Helping with the education of children by tapping into their preferred linguistic modality and submodalities
- Writing pieces that are more compelling and convincing because they create a connection between you and the audience who will read them
- Communicating better even when it happens over distance (e.g., via phone or messages).

OK, So How Do You Build Rapport?

Building rapport is the underlying common goal to everything in neuro-linguistic programming, so it only makes all the sense in the world that we will dedicate a special section to this, especially after having introduced you to the absolute basics of how NLP specialists perceive communication.

To understand just how important rapport is in NLP, imagine that it is the one ingredient the NLP recipe can't miss—the tomato sauce in the pizza, the cocoa in the chocolate, the sugar in carbonated drinks.

To define it in simple terms, rapport is a way of building mutual respect with your interlocutors. You don't necessarily have to actually like people in order to create a rapport with them—and maybe even more importantly, you don't turn your rapport on and off. The rapport you build with people should flow in a constant way.

In neuro-linguistic programming, you should establish rapport before you even expect your interlocutor(s) to listen to you, regardless of who they might be, what the context may be, or what the goal of the communication may be.

Unfortunately, there is no "Access Rapport" button you can instantly switch on at will whenever you need it. You have to build trust and emanate integrity to be able to create this type of connection with people.

To understand what rapport is, let's go back to its very origins, in the French language, where the root word of "rapport," *rapporter* has different meanings.[5] In a nutshell, however, the French *rapporter* can refer to something that cannot be returned or brought back.

In English, *rapport* is defined as a two-way connection of sympathy and understanding.[6] When rapport has been established, you have a complete sense of trust and you can communicate freely, knowing that your message gets across and that you are getting honest, valid responses from the person(s) in front of you.

---

[5]Larousse, É. (2019). Définitions : rapporter - Dictionnaire de français Larousse. Retrieved 22 July 2019, from
https://www.larousse.fr/dictionnaires/francais/rapporter/66519?q=rapporter#65769
[6] RAPPORT | meaning in the Cambridge English Dictionary. (2019). Retrieved 22 July 2019, from
https://dictionary.cambridge.org/dictionary/english/rapport?q=rapport+

Most of the time, establishing rapport is fairly easy when it comes to people who are *like you*; they either like the same things or pertain to a group you pertain to (be it work-related or not).

Unfortunately, though, most of the people you will come in contact with and communicate with are not necessarily like you. They respond to different types of communication, and your job as a good communicator is to make sure you adjust to their language.

The great news is that yes, rapport can be built even with people who are not like you. Even more, it can be built with people you don't particularly like or dislike either. And the best part about it is that it can save you so much time and energy that it is more than worth pursuing it!

Don't be quick to label people you don't naturally establish rapport with as "difficult." Like yourself, their brains have created their own mind maps and, as such, they react to the world around them according to the software they have been programmed on.

As someone familiar with neuro-linguistic programming, however, you should be able to adjust to that person's mind map and language so that you can match it up and create a bridge of communication. You would be surprised at just how *not* difficult that person can become when you are on the same page as them!

In order to get there, however, it is not enough to know the *theory* behind rapport and everything it entails. You need to make sure that you show genuine interest in people. Open your mind and your heart and try to understand the ways in which they function. Try to understand their beliefs, their values, the things that have shaped their metaprogramming into what it is today. Try to understand if they are the kind of people who are more prone to respond to visual stimuli or auditory stimuli, for example.

Although there is no "set recipe for success" when it comes to reading the people around you, there are some things you can do. For instance, you can follow a pattern of reading people so that you can make more sense of their metaprogramming and how you can adjust to that. The pattern can include the following tips of information:

- Their name
- The company they work for or the group they pertain to

- Your relationship to them
- How you want to alter your relationship with them
- How this change would impact your life
- If the impact is worth the energy you will invest in this process
- The things that might be pressing this person
- The things that are important to this person
- Do you know someone who has already built a rapport with them, and can you talk to them?
- Based on the information you have gathered, what do you plan on doing next?

We are more than certain that you will, sooner or later, reach a simple conclusion: Rapport matters a lot in the vast majority of cases.

Why?

Because building rapport is all about building relationships. And building relationships is precisely what lies at the very core of every type of success in life. A happy marriage is built on a great relationship. A thriving career is a collection of relationships you create and nourish over the course of your work years. A fit body is a good relationship with your body and your mind.

If we have to refer to the professional field only, you probably know by now just how crucial networking can be. According to studies, only one in four people don't network at all.[7] Even more, a staggering 85% of all jobs are filled through the power of networking.[8] And networking cannot actually happen without establishing rapport. Again, you don't have to actually like the person you are building rapport with, just like you don't have to actually like every single online customer your eCommerce store brings in. However, you should establish a relationship based on mutual respect and efficient communication in order to move forward with pretty much every person you meet in life.

---

[7][Infographic] - 6 Statistics On Networking And Steps For Future Success | Ryze. (2019). Retrieved 22 July 2019, from https://ryzeapp.co/infographic-six-statistics-on-networking/
[8][Infographic]: the importance of face to face networking. (2019). Retrieved 22 July 2019, from https://www.virgin.com/entrepreneur/infographic-the-importance-of-face-to-face-networking

For example, when you go to an interview, you want to establish rapport with the person in front of you by bringing the communication on your grounds—the grounds you can control and feel safe within. At the same time, you don't want to be obvious about this, so you will naturally establish a connection with the person in front of you, maybe crack a joke of some sort, smile, and display an honest, positive attitude in general.

Many times, rapport does not come in a natural way. It's hard work, and yes, it might mean that you will have to do some thorough research on the people you meet before you do so. Learning what makes people tick can be tricky, but there are many out there who have built an entire career out of this and love it (e.g., that is precisely what excellent marketers do!).

Some of the ways in which you can boost your rapport-building skills include the following:

- Be genuinely interested in the person you communicate with. Don't be interested just because you want to reach your end goal. Instead, be interested in this person because they are fascinating, because they are complex, because, just like you, they are a human being, but unlike you, their metaprogram works differently than yours does.

- If you notice someone using certain words or phrases more often, pick them up and try to naturally include them in your communication. Don't try to imitate, but use these words naturally, as this can help you start building a bridge between you and the person in front of you.

- Observe how people like to handle their information. Do they want a lot of detail, or do they just want the main idea? When you deliver your message, try to do it similarly to what they would like to hear in terms of the sizing of the communication.

- Observe how this person uses their representational systems and the type of language they are more inclined to use, and then include the same linguistic modalities and predicates in your own communication as well.

- Try to breathe at the same time this person is breathing. Yes, this might be a bit odd, so it is important to be subtle. However, breathing in the same rhythm might actually help you tune in to how they are feeling at the moment so that you can match that up in your communication.

- Observe the tone of voice, the speed with which someone talks, their gestures, their body language and try to mirror them in a way that feels natural (rather than just an imitation).

- Try to determine the person's actual intentions and aims. Sometimes, people say one thing, but do a completely different thing, which shows that there is a disruption between their communication and their actual goal. It is important to be aware of this, but it is even more important to start with the reasonable doubt presumption and assume that the heart of the person in front of you is in the right place.

When this is not the case, it is more than likely that what these people say will matter only in a very small percentage. Their message will come across to you not through articulate language, but through body language more than anything.

There is no exact science to knowing when someone lies. But you might notice that someone's words are not congruent to their actual goals because they block you out, because their eyes avoid yours, or because they have a general state of unrest to them that gives them away.

Of course, there are also people who are very good at lying. But the better you are at reading people in general, especially using NLP, the more likely it is that you will be able to easily spot these people when they pop up in front of you.

A Brief Review of Neuro-Linguistic Programming

The entire first part of this book has been dedicated to helping you understand what NLP is, where it sprang from, and how it can actually help you achieve a better self.

Look at this part of the book as a theoretical one. Although we have offered you a good bunch of examples and some exercises too, we haven't gone in-depth with the actual NLP techniques used for self-improvement. This is what the second part of this book will be dedicated to.

Before we jump headfirst into what we believe to be ten of the single most important NLP strategies, let's disseminate and re-evaluate all the theory you have assimilated thus far. Moving forward, we will focus on the actual strategies and applications of NLP that you can bring into your life, but before we do that, it is quite important to make sure that the information behind the actual action is well-cemented in your conscious memory.

Neuro-linguistic programming is, simply put, a self-development approach that was developed at the middle of the 20th century based on information and theories that were already available, but more than anything, based on observation.

The basic starting point of the entire NLP theory is the fact that our brains are "programmed" to think a certain way, to see life a certain way, and to actually act upon that worldview, or world map, as NLP specialists call it.

Don't worry, this is not a theory about aliens who have programmed humans to think according to an evil master plan. The "programs" (or, better said, *metaprograms*) neuro-linguistic programming speaks about are involuntarily built by your own brain through the prism of a variety of factors.

Unlike the traditional communication model, the NLP communication model considers more than just external interferences. In fact, neuro-linguistic programming focuses almost exclusively on what specialists in the field consider to be *internal* interferences in communication—the internal processes your brain has created and relied on to make sense of all the information coming toward it on a daily basis. And, as we were saying throughout the book, there is *a lot* of information the brain has to process every day, while its capacity is of only five to nine bits of information at once.

These internal processes are all based on three main actions the brain takes when encountering information:

- Deletion - focusing on some information but completely ignoring and deleting other pieces of information
- Distortion - overlapping information on pre-existing patterns and distorting it according to them
- Generalization - overlapping a specific bit of information over a bit of information that is similar to a certain point, but not necessarily in all of its complexity

Whether the brain applies deletion, distortion, or generalization is decided by the metaprogram built into it. Look at this as the "operating system" of your brain, the same as Windows is the operating system for PCs and Mac OS is the operating system for Apple computers.

Just like with actual computer operating systems, there is not *one* engineer behind them but a multitude of them. In your brain's metaprogram, a variety of factors have made their own mark:

- Your tendency to be extroverted or introverted, depending on the context
- The values that lie at the core of your life
- The beliefs you have adopted
- The attitude you have toward something in particular (such as work) or in general (such as life as a whole)
- The memories you have, which can overlap on current experiences
- The limiting decisions you took in your past, which are currently affecting your worldview

Your senses are a very important element to consider in NLP, too. Most people use the VAK dimensions (visual, auditory, and kinaesthetic dimensions) to make sense of the world around them. Some might not use sensory language in their communication, but most of the time, when people are passionate about what they do, they are more likely to slip in various elements of sensory information.

In addition to the spoken language (be it sensory or not), body language can be self-explicit, and it can be truly eye-opening in those cases where the words of a person are not congruent with their actual purpose.

Building rapport with other people is the very essence of everything NLP advocates for. It is the core idea without which neuro-linguistic programming simply does not make sense.

And all the concepts we have relayed to you over the course of the first part of this book, they are all about building rapport. Knowing all of these things will eventually help you create a better bridge of communication—both with yourself and with other people.

The following chapter is entirely dedicated to actual techniques you can use to improve yourself and create a thriving, fearless, victorious life, which is nothing less than what you truly deserve!

CHAPTER 8:
10 NLP TECHNIQUES FOR A BETTER SELF

As mentioned before, the first part of the book at hand has been focused heavily on the underlying theory behind neuro-linguistic programming: what it is, where it comes from, and how to work with its basic concepts.

From here on out, we are going to focus on the more practical side of things and the strategies you can use to make this work for you. Do keep in mind that you are already familiar with some of the strategies we will point out later. However, this chapter is all about actual applications and how these strategies could play out in your life.

Also, do keep in mind the fact that the strategies we will explain here are only some of those NLP practitioners use. There are many more, but our goal is to show you some of the most important and most common ones so that you can make the best use of them.

We will move with you through strategies that are easy, as well as strategies that are a bit more complex. Don't be scared of the latter ones—once you understand the basics behind them, you can definitely win the game, regardless of what your main goal may be.

So, without further ado, let us dive into the most popular neuro-linguistic programming strategies out there to see how they can pan out for you.

Strategy 1: Mirroring

We have discussed this strategy before in this book; it's just that we didn't refer to it as mirroring. Some specialists overlap NLP mirroring and NLP matching as they are quite similar in nature.

NLP mirroring means mirroring your interlocutor's movements so that you can establish rapport with them. Of course, this is not to be done in an obvious way because, yes, it could actually upset those who actually notice what you are doing.

Mirroring is a technique that involves exactly what its name suggests: taking the same actions as your partner of communication as if you were their mirror. For instance, if they move their left hand, you should move your right hand, and vice versa.

Some of the actions you could mirror include their posture, their language, the way they phrase their sentences (are they long or short?), their tone, their volume, their speed of speech, their gestures, and even their breathing pattern.

According to NLP specialists, breathing is extremely important because it puts you in tune with the person in front of you on a very deep level. When you breathe the same as someone else, you are more likely to feel their pulse and to be fully aligned with them, and thus, to establish the much-desired rapport. To follow someone's breathing pattern, follow their shoulders, their stomach, and their chest and how they move so that you can mirror that. Remember, of course, that you shouldn't be too obvious about this. Can you imagine the situation you would create if you let yourself intensely stare at the chest of a lady, for example?

The behaviors you should mimic and mirror should be subtle. Large movements shouldn't be mirrored. Instead, focus on the smaller things—the ones your communication partner does unconsciously, most likely. Repeat the same actions in a subtle way, as if they are unconscious on your end as well.

Your interlocutor will not notice that you are mirroring them. However, they might feel, on a deeper level, that you are of the same "herd" and that you are to be trusted. Even if you have known a person for five minutes, this technique can make them feel as safe with you as they would with their friends from childhood.

Accents are a very debated characteristic to mimic. Some people believe that this might help with establishing rapport, but when the person in front of you knows for a fact that you don't speak in their accent (because there is literally no reason to), things can very easily go downhill. Even more so, if you cannot mimic accents very well, it will be easily noticeable that you are not truly of the same origin as them, and that might be downright offensive.

Another form of mirroring is when you imitate the words someone says. For example, if they say "yes," you can approve by saying "yes" as well. If they say "you see…," you can reply back with "I see." Things like this should be done subtly too, of course; otherwise, you just risk making the person in front of you doubt your trustworthiness.

When mirroring someone's language, you might want to focus on predicates. As mentioned in the first part of the book at hand, predicates are extremely important in NLP because they provide you with the shortest bridge to rapport. As also mentioned before, try using words that pertain to the same sphere—such as visual, auditory, or kinesthetic words.

The main reason mirroring works is because, at a very unconscious level, we all like being around people who are like us. It's the same reason we tend to flock toward like-minded people, those who might like the same music or have the same hobbies as us. In diaspora communities, people of a certain nationality tend to flock together as well precisely because there is that sense of belonging that you feel from being with those who are like you.

Mirroring works because it taps into this unconscious need of ours. When you align your tone of voice, your breathing, or your language patterns with those of the person in front of you, they will unconsciously perceive you as one of their own. And, as a result, you will establish rapport.

Just think of it: You might feel really disgusted if you saw a spider or a centipede walking all over you (or even close to you), even if they are not poisonous. However, you might not feel disgust at all when you see a chimpanzee.

That is mainly because on a deep, unconscious level, chimps look much more similar to you. (It also helps that they don't crawl all over you in the middle of the night, but if you think of it, chimpanzees too can be quite aggressive so you would theoretically have reasons to fear them.)

Let's think of another example: When you are in school, you are much more likely to feel comfortable around people who are similar to you. That is precisely why high school cliques still function, for better or for worse.

Evolutionarily speaking, we are programmed to be like this because it used to provide us with safety. Back when human beings were just starting to group out, they were doing it for two main reasons. One, it was safer for them to stick to a group, and two, it was easier to procure food as well.

Like it or not, this has stayed with us in our DNA. This is why it is said that "humans are social animals." Even the least sociable person will still seek out some sort of human interaction. Only a very, very small number of people don't do it, and those cases are quite complex from a psychological point of view (e.g., in some cases, there might be some sort of trauma or depression associated with their complete withdrawal from society).

Finally, as a last example, think of how you feel when you are in a foreign country and pass by two people who speak your native language. Don't you feel like you belong with them, almost as if you would want to start a conversation with them?

The main goal of NLP mirroring is to convince your communication partner's subconscious mind that you are similar to them (even if you are the two most opposite people on Earth, this can actually work!). Slowly, the person in front of you might actually start to like you (and they might not even be able to put their finger on *why*).

Our suggestion is to not start mirroring right away. First, take your time to engage with the other person. Notice their body language, and notice your body language too. In the end, you might notice that you have already picked up some of the gestures they use in the discussion (e.g., you might have more or less unconsciously chosen to position your hands the same way).

When you are fully comfortable with someone, you might mirror them unconsciously. But when you are still not acquainted with the person in front of you and when you might not feel fully safe with them, you might have to jump-start the rapporting process and mirror them artificially.

Remember, though, just because this is an artificial mirroring, it doesn't mean that it is OK to mirror them all of the sudden. You cannot just start copying their gestures or their tone of voice and cadence of words. Do it step by step, as if to introduce yourself to their subconscious.

If the person in front of you changes one of their gestures, you should do the same, but be sure to leave a bit of delay between their change and yours so that it all looks natural and doesn't trigger their mistrust in you.

One way you can test your mirroring and whether or not it works is by introducing a new gesture on your end. You might be surprised because the person in front of you might actually copy you unconsciously. If that happens, it means you have established rapport with them and that your mirroring technique has worked.

OK, so how does this help you?

Well, imagine you can connect with anyone, at any time, in a matter of minutes. Imagine you can make everyone trust your words entirely because they feel that you two belong to the same clique. Imagine how that would work in sales, marketing, public speaking, and pretty much every other professional field you can actually think of. Imagine how that would work in dating!

The possibilities are, without a doubt, endless.

Yes, you should not abuse this strategy, especially since it can be very tricky to mirror someone without making them feel imitated or downright mocked.

Yes, the words you say are obviously important in any kind of communication. You can't ask your workmate to give you a sheet of paper when, in fact, you want a tablet. But beyond words, there are behaviors and gestures that transcend the power of any language.

We probably don't know how the first communication went between Christopher Columbus and the natives he met in the Americas. But we can logically assume intention and body language played a big part in it.

How about matching?

Well, as mentioned before, some NLP specialists say that matching and mirroring are one and the same.

We tend to be on the other side of the fence here—we believe there is a distinction to be made between the two. The difference is small, but like all small differences, it can make all the difference in the world!

Specifically, the main distinction to be made between mirroring and matching lies in the fact that the first means that you mimic the gestures of the person in front of you as if they were your mirroring image (so your right hand will correspond to their left one, and so on). Matching, on the other hand, is more about the same-side mimicking, so when the person in front of you moves their right arm, you would move your right arm as well.

Another distinction that is frequently made lies in the time required for you to proceed with the mimicking. For instance, in matching, if someone does something, you would follow in at some time after (to match their actions and gestures, instead of imitating them almost on the spot).

Some specialists also make a distinction between different types of matching:

- Crossover mirroring - matching one of the behaviors you exhibit to a corresponding one in your communication partner. For example, if they are tapping their fingers, you could blink in the same rhythm as their rapping.
- Mismatching - doing the exact opposite as the person in front of you. This technique is not used to establish rapport, but it is frequently used when you want to end a conversation. For instance, if someone talks a lot and you want the conversation to end, you might do the opposite of what they are doing and slow down everything about your behavior (your blinking, your breathing, etc.).

All in all, mirroring (and matching) can prove to be useful tools when it comes to creating rapport with someone. It has to be subtle, and we need to re-emphasize this as boldly as we can. But if you do it right, it might just work out for you and be the small, simple technique that will actually win people over to your side when you need it the most.

Strategy 2: Anchoring

Anchoring is a bit more complex in nature than mirroring, but it is more than worth learning about it and then applying it in your own life just to see what a huge difference it can make.

Anchoring is about your senses more than anything— sounds, sensations, smells, and so on. It is about controlling your inner core and not allowing negative communication to dictate everything you are and everything you do.

This strategy can help with a lot of issues including controlling your anger when you feel that you have been wronged or overcoming stage nerves so that you can pull off flawless presentations. Furthermore, anchoring can help a lot in those situations where past events and future events start taking over your present moment and anxiety and depression start to sink in and prevent you from being able to fully function in the present moment.

Anchoring is precisely what you need when you realize you have behaved irrationally in certain circumstances. For example, if your boss says something that instantly triggers you (even if that was not their intention), you might react very badly to this; in fact, you might even lash out on them. Later on, you might realize that you overreacted and think that something came over you.

When applying anchoring as a strategy in the above types of situations, the likelihood of everything degenerating into something really awful is much, much slimmer.

Truth be told, we are all bound to have a variety of emotional responses in a variety of situations. Emotions are precisely what makes life very, very interesting. They are what make us human and wonderful at the same time. However, the main issues arise when your emotional responses are way over the energy threshold of the message you have received. When you have piled emotion over emotion, things can easily get out of hand when it comes to your reactions—and that is where anchoring can help.

In NLP, the way you feel at a given moment is called a "state." The anchoring technique is very tightly connected to the concept of "state." When these states are taken to extremes, they can wake up very unfavorable emotions in others, and this can become an endless cycle, one only you can put an end to. If you don't put an end to them, extreme states could end your social life, your professional life, and, depending on how everything plays out, your personal life as well.

It's easy to see why people might not trust someone whose suddenly blows their fuse. They don't see everything you went through up to that moment, all the negativity you have piled up inside. Most of them see these reactions at face value: exaggerated responses to apparently small, insignificant communication errors.

Neuro-linguistic programming anchors are tools that help you anchor yourself into a positive state when these situations arise so that you avoid the escalation of a problem. Anchors are external stimuli that help you trigger an internal response—a positive one, for that matter.

Anchors are not a new concept. Our brains set them all the time when we associate certain external stimuli with internal processes. For instance, if you think of chocolate cake right now, you might find that you are licking your lips.

The idea of helping people set anchors that stabilize their internal reactions (and external mirroring of those reactions) came from Milton Erickson's hypnotherapy techniques. According to his theory and practices, using certain cues as triggers can help you reach a certain state when needed—as if to push a button.

In NLP, there tends to be a lot of emphasis on getting both the client and the therapist in very positive states to begin with. Some specialists call these "high-performing states." So, it can be said that anchoring is one of the primary techniques used in neuro-linguistic programming, as it is the strategy from which a lot of therapists start.

Circling back to the definition and explanation of anchoring, it would probably help you to understand that one of the most famous (and one of the first) examples of anchoring is that of Pavlov's dog. Everyone knows the experiment—Pavlov used an external stimuli (food) to get the same response from his dog (salivation), and paired the sound of the bell with the stimuli. Therefore, the dog always associated the sound with the idea that he would be getting food.

Before Pavlov, Twitmyer ran another very interesting test related to anchoring. He discovered that, when he took a hammer to the knee of a subject and a bell sound was running in the background, the patient started associating the bell sound with the knee-jerking reflex of being hit by a hammer, even if the action didn't actually happen.

What this taught the scientific world is that most human beings will develop responsive behavior when they associate them with a particular stimulus. It seems that we're not the only ones on Earth that do this—dolphins, dogs, seals, chimpanzees, and even lions can be taught amazing tricks when they are exposed to certain stimuli. We will not debate here whether or not this is animal cruelty—but it is something that has been practiced for a long time.

You can actually use this amazing human ability to find balance in your life too. More specifically, you can set anchors within yourself and use them when you want to reach what NLP specialists call a "resourceful state."

From the very moment you are conceived in your mother's womb, you start reacting to stimuli. It is a known fact that, for example, some babies react to their mother's voice when they are in their womb. That is, indeed, a reaction to a stimulus. So setting an anchor and turning to it as a stimulus when you need it should come pretty naturally.

Most of the anchors your brain creates are involuntary. For instance, if you have ever had one too many shots of tequila, feeling its smell might make you feel very nauseous even if it has been *years* since the unfortunate event. Likewise, if your mother always used a certain perfume when you were a kid, you might associate the smell of that perfume not only with your mom, but also with the feeling of comfort and safety you used to get when you were spending time with her.

There are three main techniques in which you can use anchors to your benefit:

- Define your positive state. Not everyone's states are the same, and your positive state might not look or feel like those of the actors in the movies who do yoga to reach those states. Define what exactly is *your* positive state before you jump into the next stage. Your positive state might be all about being bold and witty; it might be about being funny; it might be about having tons of energy or enthusiasm. Everyone is different. Define your own positivity.

- Think of a specific moment when you reached that state. What you are looking for is an experience that can be comparable to pretty much anything, even if the context behind it and the situations you are experiencing now (or will experience in the future) are very different.

- Call that experience back into your active memory. Think of every small detail: the smell, the light, the exact actions that happened, how you felt on a physical level, as well as how you felt on an internal level. Also, try to think of what you were doing with your body then (e.g., where you held your hands). Every small detail can matter, so try to bring back as much as possible.

Going back to that memory and reliving it so vividly will bring back not just the memory itself, but your positive state as well. So, every time you need to get into that positive state, you can now call back the anchor you have created for this emotion.

There is a pretty specific set of attributes all anchors should have in order to actually work for you and provide you with the positive state you are looking for. They should be:

- Special and distinctive. Everyday moments associated with their everyday movements, pictures, and sounds will not work here.
- They should be something of *yours*, something unique you have experienced.
- They should be powerful, vivid, and intense.
- They should be treated like a skill, and you should be able to actively work with them.

Our brains don't always create the best and most positive anchors in a natural way. On the contrary, it seems that we are more inclined to create negative anchors. For instance, if you are very stressed at work and come back every day in an elevated state of negativity, your dog's friendly welcome at home might end up as a negative anchor that calls back to those specific memories.

Some types of anchors are quite common among multiple people. For instance, your first day of school might have been associated by your brain with the smell of chalk and freshly polished furniture. The thing is, you are probably not unique regarding this—everyone in your class felt it, everyone in the school felt it, year after year, generation after generation. Chances are that these memories are quite common to all of those who went to school with you (and even those who went to other schools in other parts of the world!).

Establishing positive anchors is crucial to your mental balance, especially if you have been experiencing elevated, exaggerated states of mind recently. Likewise, however, it is important for you to try and avoid unwanted negative anchors. Try to make sure your negative states are not associated with anything recurring. Going back to the example given before, you could, for instance, take five minutes to relax before you enter your house and allow your dog to give you his wiggly tail welcome.

What is probably even more fascinating about anchoring is that you can use it to determine your interlocutor's state of mind as well. If you pay attention, you might discover that they are angry and that they have a certain facial expression when they are angry. This will help you calibrate your communication according to their state so that you can communicate more efficiently with them.

You might not be able to fully do this with someone you have just met, that much is true. However, you can definitely try it with your workmates, for example. You can easily notice their behavioral habits by observing how they react in certain situations or when you ask them a certain type of question. If you "record" their behavior, their gestures, their tone of voice, and so on, you will be able to access this folder in your memory when you need to discuss important matters with that workmate (or, in some situations, your boss).

For example, when you first want to get someone in a neutral state, you can simply ask them something basic and mundane—such as what they think of the weather, for example. To get them in a positive state, ask them about something or someone they like, such as the latest soccer game their team won or a type of music you know they like. Observe how they react when you ask them this question. Are they doing something in particular? Chances are that they will use that "something" in the future as well, when they are in the same positive state,

Last, but not least, briefly ask them about something they don't like—such as coffee without creamer, if you know they don't like that, for example. Notice their reactions— maybe not the most obvious ones (such as a grimace on their face, which might be very visible). Look for small hand gestures or the way they hold their eyes, for example. This might help you in the future, as well, to determine if they are in a negative state.

The applications of having this type of information at your fingertips are numerous, as you can imagine. But maybe even more importantly than that, it can completely change your perspective on how communication happens. As you will notice, communication is *there* even in the absence of actual language. Communication happens all the time. Even when people don't talk or write or use sign language, they still communicate through their behaviors, through the small gestures that say so much about where they are from the point of view of their mental state.

You too can communicate a lot without saying a single word. Sometimes, one look is enough for you to send a message about how you are feeling. Just think of the very sad moments in your life and how your closest friends knew there was something wrong with you before you even opened your mouth.

Even more so, keep in mind that you can actually use anchors to change people's states of mind too and bring the communication back to safer grounds. For instance, when someone is in a negative state, you might learn that changing your tone of voice or briefly mentioning something that person likes will bring them to better feelings.

Anchors can be extremely useful for anyone in all aspects of life. They can be useful when you give a presentation and want to change your audience's state (e.g., make them feel touched, excited, etc.). They can help when you have a one-on-one with your boss. They can help when you want to convince your workmate to do something with or for you. And, ultimately, they can help calm down the spirits at home, too, when you return to your loved ones.

One anchor might not be enough for you to "access" whenever you need it. Ideally, you want to build an entire portfolio of them and pull out the right one at the right moment. You might need an anchor for when you have to speak publicly, an anchor for those moments when you need to be at your very best and most convincing state, and another anchor for those moments when you have to deal with personal issues.

If you want anchors to work out on you and on those you interact with, you have to start by knowing yourself very well. You have to know what those triggers are that take you back to positive states. Sometimes, it might be a simple sound—like arranging crayons in a box. Other times, it might be a more complex memory—like the first date you had with your loved one and how happy you were that they accepted to go out with you.

Everyone is different, and everyone is triggered by different stimuli—be they positive or negative. Knowing yourself is the first stage in winning the anchoring game.

As Socrates himself said it, *know thyself* is the key to a good existence.[9]

Remember that anchoring is not a tool you buy from the supermarket and then simply use. It is something you have to work for. It will take some time for you to figure out the right anchors for yourself. And it might take some time for you to learn how to bring them back into your active memory as well.

The main idea is that anchoring is pure science. As we mentioned in the beginning of this section, all human beings are conceived to react to stimuli even before they are actually born—and they maintain the same wonderful capacity throughout their adulthood as well. If you can learn how to use this, you will be a much calmer, happier person. But maybe more than anything, you will be a person who knows how to influence others and a person who is simply taking the better, less emotional, and more rational decisions.

---

[9]Socrates: Know Yourself. (2019). Retrieved 15 July 2019, from https://www.the-philosophy.com/socrates-know-yourself

Strategy 3: Reframing

Reframing is also known as "content reframing" in the NLP world. Sometimes, it is also referred to as a "meaning reframe." All these terms call back to essentially the same thing: one's ability to turn negative behaviors into positive ones.

No, this is not anything like waving a magic wand and simply pulling out a positive behavior out of the hat. Just like with most NLP techniques, it might take a bit of hard work for you to master it, but as you will see in this section, all the effort is more than worth it.

There are three main stages to reframing:

- You find an alternative to satisfy your positive intent
- You negotiate with your own self to resolve the conflict at hand
- You check for the necessary ecology you need to implement the new behavior

Sometimes, reframing is used not only to change your behavior into a positive one, but also when you want to change the context of a problem.

Same as anchoring and mirroring, reframing is nothing invented. The first NLP specialists did not reinvent the wheel when they created this technique; they merely observed natural behaviors in people and synthesized those into processes that everyone can use to achieve the same results in ways that are not organic.

Reframing happens when a lot of the meaning in your day-to-day life gets lost—most often by accident, but sometimes deliberately as well. To understand how reframing works, let's define what a *frame* is, first and foremost.

A frame is a context, but it can also be your main focus for your thoughts and actions. Your beliefs, your values, your perceptions, your limitations, your skills, and a myriad of other factors build frames around specific situations in your life, and by doing this, they change the meaning of those situations. Consciously or not, you always create frames around your experiences.

While this definitely has a natural purpose in and of itself, it is quite important to acknowledge that frames can be limiting. They can completely change how you perceive an experience.

Think of this the same way as you would think of art If you take a painting that is quite dull and doesn't mean much to you, but you add a frame that has been painted by your kid, the painting will instantly gain a new meaning for you.

The same goes with your mental frames as well. They act as a point of focus for all of your thoughts and actions. As mentioned above, though, frames can be limiting as well, so it is quite crucial that you know how to work with them correctly.

Changing the frame of a situation in your life can completely change how you perceive it and how you react to said experience. For instance, if you are running late with a task, but you are told that you have two more days to complete it, this time frame will allow you to de-stress and re-focus on finishing and delivering the task. If you are told that you have two hours, however, your reaction will be completely different.

The good news about reframing is that you don't have to wait for an external factor to change your frame. If you use this NLP technique, you can reframe negative situations into positive ones on your own as well.

Content reframing starts with a couple of basic questions you need to ask yourself:

- Is there any chance this can mean something else? And if so, what is it?
- How can you turn this into a positive experience?

NLP specialists say that there are two ways a situation can be reframed: based on its content (the very meaning of that situation) or based on its context.

Let's take a look at both:

1. Content frame. This is all about what you want to focus on. Or, in another more popular term, it is all about seeing the glass half full (as opposed to seeing it half empty). For instance, if you go on vacation and realize at your destination that you have no signal on your phone, you might take this as a negative situation. But you can also reframe it and see it as a positive situation because it allows you to spend more time with your loved one(s) and disconnect from all the technology that has been clogging your life.

Likewise, you might choose to focus on the meaning you associate with some people's behavior. For instance, if your boss comes with a wet towelette and wipes the coffee ring on your office desk, you might perceive this as a passive aggressive action, when, in fact, it could be very well-intentioned. If you change the focus from what you perceive your boss to be like (based on the bosses you had before or even based on the actions of the same person you are working with now), you might find that things are far less negative than what you make of them.

Remember the basic rule behind NLP: All behaviors are born out of positive intentions. Reframing taps into this rule very directly as it works with your capacity to see the glass half full, instead of allowing negativity to take over.

2. Context reframing is all about the specific setting of a situation. For instance, it is definitely OK to go to the beach wearing swimming shorts. But it is definitely not OK to go to the office wearing the same item. When you are wearing them to the

beach, the context is perfectly aligned with your behavior and actions. When you are wearing them to the office, the context is completely off— and, as such, the meaning associated with it will be very different too.

When you reframe the context of a situation, you basically give it another meaning. You change the statement at the core of the situation by changing its context. In some ways, you can look at this sub-technique as a reorganization of your problems; you simply take them to a different context where they are not problematic anymore.

While some specialists in neuro-linguistic programming might recommend specific stages or steps that you must use when reframing, we think there is no given recipe here. Yes, you can follow the actual steps. But the main point is for you to turn your negative situations and experiences upside down and make them into something positive by changing not the situation itself (as that might be fixed in time and space), but the context or content that frames it.

In truth, this can be the main distinction between living a positive life and one that is filled with negativity!

Strategy 4: Conflicts

Whether you like it or not, conflicts are a part of life. The same as emotions, they make life more interesting—and in a very odd way, they help you enjoy the peaceful moments in life much more as well.

There are different levels of hierarchy at which conflict can take place. In NLP, these levels of hierarchy are called "logical levels" and they are categorized as follows:

- Conflicts related to identity
- Conflicts related to your beliefs and your values
- Conflicts related to your capabilities and skills
- Conflicts related to your behavior
- Conflicts related to the environment of a given situation

These levels are not there for the sake of theory only, though. If you know what level your conflict is at, then you know where to go and "look it up" to extirpate it from your life. Sometimes, these levels are referred to as neurological levels because they are somewhat similar to the actual neurological levels, as they connect to your brain and the thinking processes behind it, as well as how that connects to your body.

Let's take a closer look at the main levels of conflict so that you can understand just how easily they can tie into solutions once you have identified the type of conflict you are dealing with:

1. Identity

This might be shocking to read, but most people don't play *one* role only in the movie of their lives. People are professionals, they are parents, they are, in their own turn, children as well. Even if you are not an actor in Hollywood, you will still find that you play a lot of parts. When there is a discrepancy between the goals of one of your identities and the goals of another, you will be in conflict.

For instance, if your career takes you traveling away from home for extended periods of time (and/or very often), but your family requires you to stay home, there will be a conflict between these two identities you have assumed.

2. Beliefs/values

As we have said it before, your beliefs and your values shape your life. They shape who you are, what you do, when you do it, and pretty much every inch of your mind map.

For instance, if you believe that, as a woman, you cannot have both a thriving career and a family, your beliefs will stand in the way of achieving one goal on at least one logical level.

3. Capabilities/skills

Although there might be people who believe they are completely lacking skills of any kind, that is completely untrue. Most people have a set of skills and capabilities. The issue arises when you have all these skills but cannot put them to use. For instance, if you have learned French because you dreamed of living in Paris, you will start to be at least somewhat frustrated that you cannot get to actually use your French. In this case, you have the kind of conflict that is more connected to external stimuli rather than anything else.

4. Behavior

Your behavior is obviously extremely important when it comes to NLP. For instance, if you are passive about your goals, you will find that this type of behavior is preventing you from achieving your goals, which means that there is a conflict between what you want and what you want to do about his.

5. Environment

Your environment can also have a very powerful impact in your own life and how you reach your goals. For instance, you might frequently find yourself asking whether or not you are hanging out with the right people whenever you take a break at work. Sure, you should spend time with those people you actually like. But even so, sometimes, you might reap a lot more benefits if you hang out with people who might pertain to a more professional-focused circle.

In general, you can spot an internal conflict from a mile away because you will notice yourself (or other people, if they are the ones in conflict with themselves) saying things like "part of me wants this, but the other part wants that." This is a clear sign of an internal conflict.

NLP can help you manage conflicts as well, precisely because it has categorized conflicts in a very comprehensive way—and the sooner you know these, the more likely it is that you will be able to deal with them too.

Like all conflicts, these internal ones can reach a resolution the moment you find a compromise or a solution. It might be a solution that doesn't get you the best of the two worlds, but just as with in a relationship with a loved one, compromise is necessary when two parts are "arguing."

It is also quite important for you to take your time and get down to the deep source of a problem. Even issues that seem to arise out of nowhere are completely rooted in very specific causes.

NLP talks about internal conflicts a lot because according to this practice, most of the problems in one's life are actually related to the way they process incoming information and how absorbed emotions are dealt with. Aside from internal conflicts (also called intrapersonal conflicts), NLP distinguishes three other categories of conflict: interpersonal (between two or more people), intergroup (between two or more groups), and intragroup (between people pertaining to the same group).

Strategy 5: Calibration

Calibration can be defined as an NLP strategy that allows you to both notice and measure the needed changes in relationship to a given standard. This means that most often, two different states of external cues are to be measured.

We will not dwell too long on this specific strategy because we have touched upon it in the first part of our book here. However, we would like to give you actionable information in the second part of the book as well so that you can take the technique into your actual, day-to-day life.

What calibration does, in very brief terms, is allow you to coordinate and calibrate yourself according to the physical and behavioral cues of others and the knowledge of how they link to their internal responses (whether they are cognitive or emotional).

As human beings, we have been given the great gift of being able to make comparisons. The higher your sensory acuity is, the more you will be able to compare people, places, behaviors, and so on.

In NLP, calibration is used to help people like you who are interested in mastering the game of communication. The main goal of this strategy is to allow you to read the non-verbal, unconscious responses of others. Clearly, the benefits and applications of this are quite numerous since the technique will actually enable you to "read" people and adjust yourself and your communications according to what your reading tells you.

In general, you want to look at some very specific things you can calibrate—the modalities of calibration. They include the following:

- The tone of voice
- The volume
- The posture
- The facial color (i.e. whether they are pale, for example)
- The eyes (including the dilation of the pupils)
- Any kind of muscle tension
- How they hold their head and spine
- How they breathe

Calibration is based on working with your partner in communication and learning their specific behaviors, so that you can memorize them and use them when the time comes.

Here's a bit of an exercise to help you understand the whole concept of calibration a little better:

1. Bring your communication partner onto ground they feel safe on. Ask them to think of something they are very familiar with, something they fully understand.

2. Observe their physiology in relation to their response. Pay attention to all the details, including (but not only) the modalities of calibration mentioned before.

3. Introduce confusion. Ask your partner something that might confuse them (or something that is intentionally unclear).

4. Observe again. Analyze their reaction and physiological response to this question. Has something changed when compared to the first state you induced in them with your comfortable question?

5. Let them choose. Ask your interlocutor to choose either of the questions you have asked them and think of it again. They don't have to give you an actual answer; they should only be thinking of it.

6. Observe (again!). Has anything changed when compared to the last time they were thinking of the same question?

7. Guesswork. Based on their reaction, can you guess which of the questions they thought of? Verify with them if you are right.

8. Ask your partner to think of other concepts that they find either confusing or crystal-clear. Play around, trying to guess which category their thoughts fall under.

9. Explain one of the concepts to your interlocutor. Can you determine whether they understand it or not? Can you determine the exact moment they understand it?

Calibration takes a bit of practice, and it is important to know that not everyone has the same reaction to the same questions, even when they are very similar. In time, however, you will find it easier and easier to "read" those in front of you (and thus, to adjust yourself according to their internal responses).

Strategy 6: Meta-Models

The meta-model is a concept we briefly touched on toward the beginning of this book, but we feel that it is extremely important to know that, aside from being one of the quintessential concepts behind NLP, meta-models can be considered to be a strategy in their own right too.

In very simple terms, a meta-model is a set of questions that aims to gather specific information, challenge, or expand someone's map of the world.

Sounds like fun, right?

It is, we promise.

Meta-models are created according to the person's deletions, distortions, and generalizations (as they are noticed in their language). Ever since its inception (which goes as far back as the fathers of NLP, Grinder and Bandler), meta-models were based on general semantics and transformational grammar.

The concept of meta-modeling starts with the NLP tenant according to which language does nothing more than translate your mental state into actual words that can be used and understood by other people as well. So, language bridges what you think and feel to the world outside so that everyone can actually know what you need, feel, or want.

As we have mentioned time and again in our book here, different people react differently to certain stimuli, so it is important to notice and take note of this and create comments (mental or otherwise) to help you determine what state the person in front of you is in and, as such, to adjust your communication.

The way communication is adjusted is based on people's pictures, their sounds, their feelings. Everyone reacts to stimuli, but it is important to see exactly what the stimuli your partner of conversation is reacting to so that you can, again, adjust your communication according to this.

The meta-model is a method that helps you collect information from mental maps that are lacking in information and bring it back to sensory experiences so that you can actually see behavioral changes. Meta-models should be seen through the point of view of the three main processes that alter information in the human brain: deletions, distortions, and generalizations. For each of these processes, a different meta-model approach should be taken, as follows:

Deletions

In NLP, there are several types of deletions that might occur, and you should, again, take a different approach according to each of them.

Here are some of the main types of deletions included here:

- Simple deletions. In these cases, statements are missing important elements (e.g., "Go do it!" The most appropriate responses in these cases are to ask for more details (e.g., "Do what?"). This type of question would bring the communication back on track.

- Missing verbs. In these cases, the verb used in a statement is unclear and it doesn't say how the action leads to the result in the statement. For instance, if you say, "My dog helped me achieve this," it is quite unclear what your dog could have done for you to achieve something. To bring the communication back on track, you would have to ask about the correlation between the action and the result.

- Missing comparisons. Null comparatives, as these types of deletions are known, are comparisons in which the first element is missing or not clearly stated. For instance, you might find this on a box of cookies that says "30% more"—but the communication is incomplete because you don't know what that 30% is more *of*. More than the other brands of cookies? More than the normal amount per box of cookies for this brand? To bring the communication back on track, you would ideally have to ask for more information here. (It's unlikely that it is possible in the case of advertising, but in other types of communications, it might be possible.)

- No referential index specified. In other words, this is about using a pronoun when the context is rather unclear. For instance, if you say "She will go to the market," that "she" at the beginning of the sentence is quite ambiguous because, unless it was specified before, and unless "she" is the only "she" in a pretty wide area, it would be better if "she" was replaced with an actual name.

- Missing subject. Also known as Lost Performative, this type of deletion removes the *doer* from the statement. Or, in other words, the person who performed an action is not mentioned ("Her talent for singing is amazing"). Again, the communication has to be brought back on track with extra questions.

Distortions

Just like in the case of deletions, distortions too come in many flavors. Following, we will explain some of the most important ones. Understanding them means that you will be able to understand a very important part of the meta-model strategy so that you can truly make the most of it in your day to day life.

- Presuppositions. These are assumptions where the truth is automatically assumed (or taken for granted, if you want to put it that way).

  When it comes to presuppositions, it is crucial to keep in mind the fact that the negation of the expression does not change, in any way, its presuppositions. For instance, if you say that you will "never go there again" or if you say that you will "go there again," the presupposition is that you have already been "there," and it doesn't change regardless of whether the expression is negated or not.

Most communications include some sort of presupposition, even if it's just the fact that the person in front of you understands your language, for example. As mentioned before, a lot of the communication happens beyond the actual words we spell out, as we always communicate underlying meanings.

It is quite important to keep presuppositions in mind because they could alter the communication between us and other people. Using meta-model techniques, you can remove this risk from your communication. To do this, you will have to split a message and determine its presuppositions, as well as *who* they are true for. Doing this will allow you to be flexible in communication and challenge the other person's presuppositions as well.

For instance, if someone says, "I don't mean to upset you when I joke like this," there are several presuppositions in this expression. One is that the person saying this makes jokes that might be offensive to the recipient of the message. Another one is that the person may have made the same kind of jokes in the past.

And the list can go on and on.

The important element here is to become aware of the fact that these presuppositions may or may not be true for both you and your interlocutor. By spotting the presuppositions, however, you are able to change them and bring the communication where you want it to be.

- Cause and effect. Many people think of complex elements in very simple terms—or casual thinking, as this is sometimes referred to as. When x means y and a makes you b, you are thinking casually.

  Of course, this makes sense, and it is one of the ways in which the brain is able to cope with so much information and the many processes it has to handle.

  However, you should be quite cautious with using causality, as it may sometimes lead to distortions.

Causality means that there is a relationship of dependency between the cause and effect and that when the cause arises, the effect arises as well. However, this might not *always* be true and not in all cases—and knowing how to make the distinction between those instances when it is true and those when it isn't is precisely what lies at the foundation of emotional intelligence.

In NLP, the main causality-related effect is assuming that all of your internal states are an effect of external actions and conditions. For instance, if you feel blue one day, you might blame this on the weather outside or bad news you have heard over the radio on your way to work.

Causality can distort your experience because it eventually makes you believe that all of your internal states (be them positive or negative) are automatically related to an external cause. As you can probably imagine, this can only lead to unhappiness because when you base your joy and your sorrow strictly on what happens outside of you, there is a risk that you will never take control over your life.

Meta-modeling can help you move past the cause and effect patterns you have established within yourself. Challenging yourself, the speaker, to think about the relationship between your states and the external events and stimuli will help you take control over what happens inside of yourself.

Every time you find yourself saying things like "my job is too stressful," "you make me feel sad," or even "this dreadful, rainy weather makes me feel too down," stop for a moment and think about it. What happens internally can only be controlled internally. You cannot control other people's annoying habits, the level of stress you have to endure at work, or even more, the weather. But only you can control what happens within yourself and how you react to all these external events and stimuli.

Think of what exactly makes you feel stressed out, for example, instead of simply blaming it on your "work" in general. Think of how someone makes you feel sad or upset. Think of just how absurd it is that you want *weather* to change its course just so that you can feel yourself.

If you take these things into consideration and think about them, you will most likely be able to stop the negative pattern that has been plaguing you. The moment you recognize you are in control of your emotions is the moment you stop allowing everything on the *outside* of your brain to control what happens with you.

- Mind reading. Obviously, nobody can read minds. There might be people who are very good at reading nonverbal communications and contexts and making deductions on what someone may be thinking (which is what NLP can teach you as well, especially at the more advanced levels). But nobody can enter anyone's mind and see exactly what is in there.

  In NLP, the mind reading violation is a distortion that can be handled with the help of metamodeling. This so-called "mind reading" happens when someone simply claims they absolutely know, without hesitation, what another person is thinking (and they do not even verify or validate their theory).

For instance, if you instantly assume, when thinking about a specific couple, that "if she continues to be such a slob, he will eventually leave her," you are in the wrong. You are instantly assuming, based on nothing more than speculation, that "he" cares about her sloppiness or that this is a decisive factor for him like it might be for you, for example.

If you happen to stumble upon someone who might be this type of mind reader, or if you notice that you might have this type of communication pattern embedded in your behavior, stop for a moment and ask: What made you arrive at that conclusion? Is the information you have (or the information someone else has) correct and whole?

- Nominalization. If you look up the word, you will most likely see that it has multiple meanings. This time, however, we are not discussing nominalization in the sense of "nominating someone."

Perhaps unsurprisingly for neuro-linguistic programming, the nominalization meaning we are dealing with here is related to, well, language. In NLP, specialists consider that nominalization occurs when a verb becomes a noun—and, as such, a dynamic action or process becomes something static.

Normally, there should be no problem with this. However, when you "stop" the action and only consider the point at which you have stopped it, you might not get the bigger picture. Or, in other words, you might find yourself facing an incomplete communication.

For instance, if someone says, "I have to make a decision by Thursday," you might not know what decision (from the verb "to decide") that is if you have no context.

Do keep in mind that nominalization does not necessarily occur every time a verb becomes a noun. To determine if nominalization has happened, there are two main tests you can run:

o   The wheelbarrow. If you can put the object relayed by the word in a wheelbarrow and actually carry it around, it is not a nominalization. For instance, "to drink" generates "drink." However, "drink" is not a nominalization because you can actually put that drink in a wheelbarrow.

○ If you can use "continuous" with your supposed nominalized word, then it IS a nominalization. For instance, "breath" comes from "to breathe," and if you use "continuous breath," it will make sense. Ergo, "breath" is a nominalization.

What is the main problem with nominalizations?

Well, nothing and everything at the same time, too. When you turn an action into something that is frozen in time, it loses its main meaning and it can become ambiguous. Even more, when you have frozen an action in time, it means that it is already *done and gone*—which might have some pretty deep implications.

For instance, when a couple argues, and one of them says "there is no communication between us," it already implies that they have stopped communicating. At an unconscious level, the recipient of the message (i.e. the other side of the couple) will actually perceive this as it is sent, and it will escalate the issue even more.

To apply a meta-model to this type of problem, trace the nominalized word back to being a verb and ask questions about it. Circling back to the example above, turn "communication" into "communicate" and ask yourself, for instance, *who* is not communicating what and to whom?

Choosing your words carefully is, as you have probably noticed so far, extremely important. Even the wrong form of a word can communicate, at a subconscious level, the wrong message. So, before you use nominalized forms, think things through and analyze just how much they can reshape your communication.

Complex equivalence. The last type of distortion we will discuss in this book, complex equivalence, is defined as drawing unrelated conclusions from events and creating a flawed logic to support this process.

For instance, if your shoe breaks and you say, "I will end up failing that exam," you are basing this statement on nothing more than superstition. Some would call this being a "drama queen" too—and it is understandable why, because there is no actual correlation between the event that just happened and the one you predict to happen.

When making a complex equivalence, you assume that the two statements are equal and they have the same meaning. The meta-model you have to apply in these cases should challenge the correlation between the two statements.

For instance, did you fail an exam every time your shoe broke? And even more than that, was there any actual logical correlation between the two events? Did you ever fail an exam without having a broken shoe?

When you ask yourself these questions, you soon realize that your correlations are, well, uncorrelated.

Generalization

As we discussed at the beginning of this book as well, generalization is another process the brain uses to make sense of the world and, more specifically, to be able to handle all the information that comes toward it on a daily basis.

There are two main types of generalizations we would like to discuss from the point of view of NLP:

- Universal quantification. Look at any language on Earth and you will find that they all have a set of quantifying words people use to provide a more general approximation of numbers.

  When you say *"Everyone will be at the party,"* you might not mean that every single person in the company will attend the party (this rarely happens, right), but you mean that most of the people will be there.

  It makes sense to use quantifiers in a million and one situations. But in some cases, you might be tempted to characterize an entire set judging by a very small sample. Obviously, this can generate pretty big issues in communication, especially when the generalization is very broad.

The meta-model recovery questions you should use when you spot yourself thinking or speaking like this are related to challenging the *generality* of what you are saying. For instance, if you say that "I will never get this right," you could challenge the statement by asking yourself "Has there been any time I have done it right?" or "Have I missed every opportunity of making this right?"

- Modal operators. As you may remember from your days of learning grammar, modal operators are generally used to express a modal attitude (a necessity or an impossibility, for example).

For instance, when you say, "I can't do this," you are expressing a statement that uses a modal operator. Obviously, when your language seems to work only in terms of necessities and (im)possibilities, you are limiting your perspective and your mind map.

As you have probably figured out by this point, the meta-model you would apply in this case consists of questions that challenge the generalization behind modal operators. For instance, if you think you can't do something, ask yourself what is preventing you from doing it and what you can do to remove that impediment (if there is any real impediment)?

Meta-models are all about asking the right questions. In day-to-day communication, you may not always have the chance to move through so many questions before you open your mouth to say something. However, observing your language and the behavior associated with it can help you remove the negative patterns, one by one, step-by-step.

It might take a lot of conscious hard work, but once you have re-shaped your meta-models using the right questions, you can completely change your life from A to Z.

That's how huge and marvelous and important language is!

Strategy 7: Meta-Programs

Meta-programming is the core, quintessential concept of NLP—one we have gotten you acquainted with ever since the first pages of this book.

Believe it or not, what we have said until now about meta-programs does not even begin to scratch the surface of just how deep these little software applications run in our lives.

We hope the section at hand will, however, help shed some (more) light on how these programs run—and maybe even more importantly, how you can *run them yourself.*

As we were saying, the first lines of code in your internal meta-program are written in your childhood, by your parents, by the teachers at school, by the culture you are brought up in. These codes might change over the course of your life, according to the experiences you are exposed to, but for now, they will help you shape your reality.

Sometimes, it takes conscious work to detach yourself from the code you have been implemented with as a child. For instance, if you grew up with parents who were very restrictive, as an adult, you might have to consciously detach yourself from the restraints of your childhood to be internally free.

Other times, these programs overwrite on their own, according to what you are exposed to. For instance, if your family was rather distant to the idea of blending with other cultures, but you eventually end up traveling a lot, this will have an effect on the program you were brought up with, and it will overwrite it with new points of view, behaviors, and attitudes.

The program you are raised in, however, will have a very heavy influence on your behavior as a child and as a teenager, and it will definitely have a say in the grand decisions you will make as you come of age. If your parents are engineers, but you have an artistic nature, your decision not to pursue your talent and dream might be very heavily connected to how you were brought up and the program your parents have (unconsciously or not) written for you.

Furthermore, the way you learn might be affected by your initial programs too. Of course, this can be shaped and reshaped as you move along in life, but your first years of school will carry with them the codes you were raised with.

There is a multitude of meta-programs people function on. Because it would take entire libraries to actually talk to each and every one of them in detail, however, we will choose to focus on a handful of them. Call them the most important or the most common ones, if you wish (but keep in mind that those that will be left out are very important too!).

Hopefully, the meta-programs we will explain here will give you a better idea of just how complex people are—and how you can decode their complexities to understand them better and deliver better communications when you are around them.

Before we dive deep into their explanations and everything they ensue, we would like to mention that all human beings use multiple meta-programs. There's no such thing as someone who only uses one meta-program. We adapt according to the contexts, situations, and people we are around, so when analyzing the person in front of you, remember to take their external factors into consideration as well. They might make all the difference in the world!

Furthermore, there is no such thing as a "bad" meta-program. Remember, as we said in the beginning, from the NLP perspective, all behaviors are positive when you look at them from the perspective of what the person behind them is trying to achieve.

As it was also mentioned in the beginning of the book you are holding here, meta-programs are, in many ways, your guide to "translating" people. Being able to understand how people function will allow you to adjust your communication accordingly.

That's the short story behind NLP's meta-programs and why they are important.

The long one?

It taps into everything humans ever wanted: to be liked, to be appreciated, to be successful, to be the kind of people other people look up to, and so on. Meta-programs and their understanding will eventually help you achieve precisely what you aim for: nothing less than greatness in whatever field where you want to achieve it.

You may be tempted to think meta-programs are based on some New-Age gibberish that doesn't make much sense and doesn't deliver results. But you couldn't be further from the truth, actually. The very beginning of what NLP specialists call meta-programs was set by Hippocrates himself nearly two and a half millennia ago. His observations revealed that there are four main temperaments: choleric, sanguine, melancholic, and phlegmatic.

This classification is still widely used, but further research has revealed that a lot of people can fall into multiple categories, according to (as mentioned before) their context and the external factors influencing their behaviors and communication.

For instance, at the beginning of the twentieth century, Carl Jung described three main psychological type categories:

- Extroverts/introverts. Extroverts are people who are always energized when they are out and about, unlike introverts, who feel much better when they are all on their own.
- Sensors/intuitors. Sensors rely their entire information gathering strategy on their five senses, while intuitors will rely on their instincts more than anything.

- Thinkers/feelers. Thinkers make their decisions based on an objective, logical analysis. Feelers, on the other hand, make their decisions on subjective values.

From Jung's conclusions, a whole new era of understanding human beings arose. The famous 16 Myers-Briggs personalities are mostly based on Jung's work, for example, and it is one of the profiling schemas used most frequently these days.

Neuro-linguistic programming meta-programs are, in some ways, personality profiles. They have gained a new edge, one that connects to the basic tenets of NLP in general (that language shapes your very existence), but at their very core, they are quite close to the Myers-Briggs personality profiles, for example.

Let's take a look at seven of the most popular meta-programs:

The Proactive vs. Reactive Meta-Programs

Understanding what a proactive and reactive meta-program is will most likely come naturally to you. Someone who is more likely to take action and move is a proactive person (or at least in that given circumstance). At the same time, someone who is more likely to wait for everything to happen is reactive (again, in that circumstance).

You will recognize the proactive person by the following traits:

- They take charge
- They get things done
- They are natural problem-solvers, even in situations where it seems that multiple fires have to be put out at once
- They are frequently seen in jobs connected to leadership, sales, or freelancing
- Their body position is usually up tight, chest and head forward
- They are more likely to call, rather than email
- They are likely to use phrases like "just do it," "go with it," "take control," and so on

You will also recognize a reactive person:

- They wait for others to take the lead
- They take action only when they feel comfortable with the timing

- They risk spending way too much time in a state of analysis
- They wait to be given tasks and instructions
- Their shoulders are usually slouched and their head is turned downwards
- They are more likely to email, rather than call
- They are more likely to use phrases like "take your time," "analyze the pros and cons," "study the data," and so on.

One of the key questions you can ask to see if someone is proactive or reactive is whether or not they find it easy to take action in new situations.

People Who Move Toward vs. People Who Move Away From

If you stop to think about it, there's a high chance you have spent a fair amount of time in your life trying to either move toward something/someone or move away from something/someone.

The simplest example here is how, on January 1 every year, people inevitably set new goals for the year ahead. A very vast majority of them aim to lose weight, for example. They join a gym, they create a diet, and they go with the flow. Because they are very enthusiastic, they see results coming in quite quickly and enjoy the spur of the moment, the little wins they have so far.

But if that momentum is lost, weight loss might stagnate very quickly. They might find their gym sessions are few and far between. They might eat out and order in more often. And before they know it, they will be back to their old habits. The weight might creep back on as well.

What happens is that when they originally set their goal and were enthusiastic about it, they had a strong inner motivation to get away from something negative in their lives (their extra weight, health issues, lethargy, and so on). However, when they lose their focus, they start to run *toward* their old habits, where they feel comfortable.

Generally, health-related actions are connected to an "away from" meta-program, as most people want to get away from the complications of poor health. However, this is not a good approach, as it will eventually make you backpedal into your old habits.

Instead, having a *toward* attitude when it comes to health and weight loss is likely to give better results in the long run—precisely because you are drawn toward a very clear goal because you are not running away from something worse, but toward something better.

In general, meta-programs are what they are, and they shouldn't be changed. But, depending on the situation (like in the weight loss and health example above), you might want to work with your *away from* meta-program and re-shape it into something that will make it more probable for you to actually reach your goals.

This is not to say that being an *away from* person is wrong. Au contraire, there are situations and roles when this type of thinking is actually beneficial. For instance, if you are a project manager, if you maintain production plants, or if you deal with important analyses, being an *away from* person can be helpful because it will help you think of all the things that might go wrong and avoid them.

As a person who tends to run away from things, you are also more likely to be motivated by negative reinforcers (such as the fear of losing your job or the consequence of not meeting your KPIs this quarter, for example).

Sometimes, people who have a *toward* meta-program are perceived as naive because they tend to jump head first into a variety of situations the *away from*-ers would calculate and over-calculate a thousand times.

People with a *toward* tendency are motivated by the positive reinforcers—such as the fact that they will continue to work on a great team or the fact that they will receive their yearly bonus if they do reach their KPIs.

The quintessential questions to ask when you want to find out if someone is a *toward* or an *away from* person go in-depth on about three levels until you see the real motivation behind someone's actions. For instance, if you ask someone what motivates them and they say job security and then the fact that they can pay their bills and not be in debt, it means that they are an *away from*.

Toward people are more likely to use words like "achieve," "obtain," "have," or "get." *Away from* people are more likely to use words like "prevent," "avoid," "remove," and so on.

Options People vs. Procedures People

The essential distinction between options people and procedures people is that the first group of people will probably actually enjoy new things (from foods to new ways of doing old things), while the latter groups will more likely need sets of methodologies in their lives.

In general, options people show the following characteristics:

- They love variety, and they will seek it as often as they can
- They start projects but rarely stick around to see them through
- They are quite good at creating procedures but not necessarily following them
- They will always drive through different routes every time, precisely because they want variety
- They are keen on testing new ways, even if there is nothing wrong with the old ones
- They do not commit easily because it feels like limiting their options and their experiences
- They are likely to say things like "playing it by the ear," "possibilities," "bending the rules," and so on

Procedure people, on the other hand, tend to show the following characteristics:

- They always prefer procedures, but they don't want to be the ones who actually create them
- They always follow a work MO, and they never skip a step of a procedure
- They always drive very safely, sticking to speed limits
- Whenever other people break the law even in the slightest bit, they will take these actions as a personal affront
- They are likely to say things like "obey the rules," "follow the steps," "finally," and so on.

The easiest way to find out if someone is a procedure person or an options one is to ask them why they bought a car. The options people will give you a list of reasons and the values that pushed them toward buying a car. Procedure people, on the other hand, will most likely list out a series of steps that got them to that decision.

Internal vs. External People

Do keep in mind that this category of meta-programs is not the same as that which describes extroverts and introverts. In this case, "external" and "internal" are two facets of how people learn new things.

External people need to be constantly reassured that they are on the right path, while internal people find that confirmation within themselves. Sometimes, the same person can switch from external to internal even when they are within the same role, with just a few of the verticals of their situation having changed.

For example, when you start a new job, you might feel the need to be reaffirmed that you are doing OK. However, as you get used to your position and role, you might find that you do not need external validation as much as you did—and as such, you will lean more toward being an internal person.

Generally speaking, entrepreneurs are rather internal. When you set up a new business, there are few indicators to validate your idea. Sure, you can test it out and yes, you can ask for opinions. But nobody can tell you exactly whether this will actually take off. As an internal person, you are OK with that, precisely because your confirmation lies within you.

Also, internal people like to do things their own way (which is one of the main reasons they are so good as entrepreneurs too). External people, on the other hand, will be much easier to work with and manage—as long as feedback is constantly given, that is.

There might not be precise words and expressions internal and external people use—but there sure are words and expressions they have a better reaction to. For instance, an internal person can be triggered by things like "only you can do this" or "see for yourself." An external one, however, is more likely to react to words and expressions like "statistics say," "this has been approved," or "experts believe that."

If you want to find out if someone is internally referenced or externally referenced, ask them how do they know they did a good job with their most recent large purchase. If they say something along the lines of "I just know," it means they are internally-focused. If they say something like "Everyone liked it," however, it means that they are externally focused.

Global vs. Detailed Persons

People are wildly different and, as such, it makes all the sense in the world that they are run by different meta-programs.

Another way you can distinguish two different, opposing meta-programs is by looking at people when they start a project. Some of them will see the bigger picture and find it easy to do so, but they might find it troublesome to go into detail as to how the big picture can be achieved. Others, however, are much better at handling the details, but they cannot necessarily see the bigger picture. The first are called "globally meta-programmed" people, while the latter are called "detailed-oriented meta-programmed" people.

How they organize their tasks is also an important distinction as well. The person with a global view will be far more likely to split their tasks into large chunks, while the person with a detailed view will definitely split them into smaller, digestible chunks.

Global people are excellent with concepts; they make for great strategists, for example. They are the kind of speech givers that will give the big idea, the big upsell, the big product (think of Steve Jobs and how he acted in his presentations at Apple, for example).

Detailed people, are, as you would expect, the kind of people who will need a lot of preparation for a speech, and they will go in a lot of detail with it. If you are listening to someone who seems to have jumped from "Good evening and welcome" straight into the details of a presentation, they are a detailed person (obviously!).

A global person can see the forest, but they will have issues managing the mass of trees in it. When there is too much information, a global person might become impatient and downright anxious.

A detailed person will, however, handle a myriad of steps as long as that is the roadmap to whatever they are aiming for—in their personal and professional lives alike. The more details, the better it is because it allows them to reconstruct the meaning of what they are doing one step at a time.

One of the main issues a detailed person might have, however, is managing the stress. Sometimes, they are paralyzed into doing nothing at all—the more the project moves on without being fully done, the more likely it is that the detailed person will disengage with the project if the tasks are not split according to their liking. When this happens, it is important to stop whatever you are doing and list your tasks, then move them around as you please to make sure all the details are in good order. This will allow you to stop procrastinating and actually get down to work.

Global people might be far more likely to use and react to words like "generally," "overview," and "seeing the big picture," while detailed people will be more likely to use and react to words like "schedule," "first," "precisely," and so on.

Preference for Sameness vs. Sameness with Difference Preference

These two meta-programs are also connected to how we learn new things. Preference for sameness means that you are more likely to match new concepts and lessons with things you already know, while sameness with difference preference means that you might have already noticed the similarities, but you prefer to spot the differences to see what is not like the things you already know.

Sameness people are usually quicker to establish rapport in their communication because they already, naturally, see the similarities between them and the person in front of them—so it is far more likely that their nerves and anxiety will settle in quicker.

Sameness people might find it quite difficult to learn new things when they have no given patterns to follow. For example, they might not learn new foreign languages very easily, especially those that are dramatically different than the rest (e.g., they might find it possible to learn Dutch, but completely out of their capacities when it comes to Russian or Chinese).

When embarking with sameness-based people on a new project, it might help if you tell them things like "I'm sure you can do this, it is similar to this previous project." The fact that there is something else they were OK with and now the same specifications are in play will help them acclimate to the idea of newness in general.

Difference-based people will definitely find it easier to learn new things precisely because they don't necessarily look up the sameness in the projects they take on. These people are likely to be heard saying things like "better," "evolution," "increase," and so on.

At the same time, however, people who are more inclined toward sameness will use words like "similar," "static," and "identical."

Past, Present, or Future Oriented

We focus differently on different dimensions of our lives. For instance, for some of us, it makes all the sense in the world to be surrounded by a pleasant environment (at home and at work). For others, however, this doesn't matter as much.

Since time is one of the most important dimensions of human life (if not *the* most important one), it only makes sense that different people have different perspectives on time.

The way you focus on time and its flow can be a meta-program in itself. In fact, NLP specialists distinguish three main categories of people here: Those who are focused on the past, those who are focused on the present, and those who are focused on the future.

None of these meta-programs are bad or good; they all come with their ups and downs. The most important thing, however, is that you learn how to control those "downs" so that you can reap more benefits when the "ups" are in place.

Focusing on the past can be odd for many, but there are a lot of people who do it. On the positive side, doing this means that you have a unique appreciation for traditions and history. You respect the elderly. You know who you are, where you come from, and what that means for you. You have a strong core set of values and beliefs.

On the negative side, however, if you focus a lot on your negative past experiences, you risk becoming bitter, full of regret and anger. You risk losing your optimism and risk missing out on living in the moment. Even more, you might find it extremely difficult to make any kind of decisions.

Focusing on the present means that you know how to take every task by its horns and get it done. It also means that you can keep your eyes on today and enjoy it to the maximum. On the downside, those who focus on the present tend to be bad learners when it comes to past lessons. What's more, those who are focused on the present rarely make plans for the happiness of their future—which can in itself be a problem.

Last, but not least, are the future people, of which there can be of two types. There are the moderate ones who always plan ahead and move through life with a good dose of optimism in their baggage. And then there are the more extreme ones for whom life happens on fast-forward because they are always rushing for some sort of "tomorrow." While it is perfectly fine to always be excited about the future, do keep in mind the fact that it is not the only perspective you have.

Each of these categories of people are likely to use certain words. Some examples include:

- Past focused: "When I was younger," "remember when," "back then," etc.
- Present focused: "It's the way it is," "what's happening is this," etc.
- Future focused: "I will," "When…," and so on.

Aside from the language you can use to determine if someone is past, present, or future oriented, there are also a series of tips that will help you deal with each of these categories better and establish actual rapport with them in your communication:

- If you are talking to someone who is focused on a negative past, agree with them and offer them your empathy. However, try not to get caught in the story itself so that you can help lead them into a better state of mind.

- If you are the one who might focus too much on the past, the present, or the future, simply shift your attention a bit. You will have to do this consciously at first, but soon enough it will come naturally. For instance, if you are caught in a past memory, shift your focus to the present by taking a good look around you and seizing every sensation and every single person and element of your current context.

Using Your Meta-Programs

There are different ways to use meta-programs.

You can use them to see how they apply to others and adjust your communication to their meta-programs. And, in the end, you can also use them on yourself, to help yourself release all negative emotions. But even more than that, you can use meta-programs to un-limit your limiting decisions—because, if you haven't heard it yet, the sky is really the only limit you have and there's no reason why you should let your natural "programming" set any kind of border as to how far you can reach.

Combining different meta-programs is a natural mechanism for many. For instance, if you work as a manager, you will be proactive and detail oriented at work, you will focus on differences, and you will want to lean toward preferences. But when it comes to how you behave at home where it's just you and your spouse or significant other, you might be the complete opposite. You might be reactive, you might be global, and you might focus more on sameness than on difference.

To develop your meta-programs in the right direction and learn how to take control over them, try to ask yourself the following questions:

- What are the meta-programs you are running now?
- What are the areas you are running them in?

- What areas would you like to improve?
- Are there areas of your life where you display good behavior but don't display the same behavior in other areas of your life?

The applications of meta-programming can run very deep. From HR recruitment to improving your relationship with your loved one, having a thorough understanding of the basic meta-programs can definitely help—and by a lot!

Strategy 8: Self-Nurturing

Neuro-linguistic programming is, without a doubt, a practice that focuses on communication. Yet, more often than not, people only see communication as an act that happens between themselves and other people.

In fact, communication happens all the time even when there is nobody else around yourself. You may not fully realize this, but you are doing it all the time: when you decide what to eat in the morning, when you wonder if you will ever be able to turn in that report on time, and before you go to sleep when you rewind, unwind, and prepare for tomorrow.

Sadly, not all the communication we "perform" on ourselves is positive.

How many times have you admonished yourself this week?

How many times have you told yourself you're not enough?

How many times have you put yourself down, perhaps inadvertently?

Chances are that you did all these things (and more) one too many times. And chances are that you are fully aware of the fact that doing this to yourself *cannot* be healthy in any way.

Just think about it: Would you say those things to someone you liked at least a little bit?

Probably not—and chances are that you wouldn't tell that to someone you deeply dislike.

But doing this to yourself is easy, especially when, at the other end of the communication line is…none other than your own self.

Establishing a proper bridge of communication with your own self is absolutely crucial. Not only will you build a better relationship with yourself (and thus, be able to move mountains), but it will help you communicate better with others too.

When you get along with your inner self, you can actually move past the boundaries of your own world map and enter those of others, touch them, change their course, and bring communication into your own realm of goals.

Self-nurturing (or self-compassion, as it is sometimes referred to) is an important NLP strategy both from the point of view of what it can help you build within yourself and from that of what it can help you build with others.

Unfortunately, it is sometimes harder to self-nurture than to nurture others. You can never know every single thing about everyone else (not even those who are your closest friends and family members, actually). But, like it or not, you know everything about yourself—consciously or not.

Self-nurturing is not something you simply wake up with one day, sadly. Just like physical fitness and mental sharpness, self-compassion happens when you work hard for it. It's a muscle you have to flex again and again until it's strong enough to carry your entire inner being into a state of balance and beatitude.

Following, we will show you two exercises you can try to "work out" your self-nurturing muscles. They are, obviously, not the only ones, but they are the easiest first steps you can take toward true self-compassion.

The Character Game

Self-criticism is an inherently human condition. For many people, it is a moderate apparition that pulls them down every now and again when they feel stressed, when they face new challenges, or when they are down in the dumps.

For many, however, self-criticism is a real issue because it doesn't pop up ever so rarely; instead, it becomes a permanent state of mind. And how can you "win" anyone over to your side when you cannot even win yourself?

The "Character Game" is an exercise you can practice when you want to achieve self-nurturing, so that you can create more balance in your self-communication.

To engage in this exercise, follow these steps:

1. Find a quiet, comfy place. Make sure nobody will disturb you for the next five to ten minutes and that you can be alone with your own thoughts.

2. Think of five characters you love and cherish. We are calling them "characters" not because they should be fictional, but because they can be anyone and anything that brings you comfort: your parents, your friends, relatives, workmates, your dog or your cat, the toys you used to play with as a kid. The one condition is that they are characters you genuinely cherish and respect no matter what.

3. Think of a situation that would normally make you feel extremely anxious. Think about it thoroughly and allow yourself to deep-dive in this context. Allow it to take over your senses and your thoughts. Think about how this makes you feel at a very honest level and put it in an actual sentence (e.g., "I feel extremely anxious about the meeting with the stakeholders; it makes me feel weak in the knees").

4. Take a brief moment to step out of the situation you have just pictured and think of the fact that there are *many* other people out there in the wide

world who feel the exact same way you do. No matter how unique your situation may be, there is at least a handful of people, at any given second, who feel the same way you do.

5. Think of them and how, even if you don't know them, you can connect to them through the same vibrations you share, the same type of anxiety, the same sensations you experience when you are in situations like the one you have just pictured. Empathize with all these people who feel the same and wish them all the best in the world. Imagine them wishing you well too.

6. Bring forward the characters you chose at the beginning of the exercise. Imagine them telling you that it will all be alright, that you need to be kind to your own self, and that you need to take care of yourself regardless of what happens. Repeat the words they are saying and internalize them. Accept their words as the rules by which you want to live in your relationship with your own self.

7. Once done, tune into your emotions and see how you feel. Do you feel anything different? Be completely honest about it and accept whatever you are feeling, whether good or bad. Draw a conclusion about what you can do to make yourself feel

better in the future—it doesn't have to be a life-changing A-HA! moment, it can be something small but meaningful.

8. Come back into your physical reality and try to actually apply the lesson you have just learned.

The Childhood Memories

The second exercise you can try when you want to practice self-nurturing is a bit more complex, but it can bring a very large array of benefits, so it is more than worth giving it a try.

Unlike with the previous exercise, this one might require some props: either a pen and a sheet of paper or some sort of digital tool that allows you to create charts or tables. It can be anything you are comfortable with. If you think you will do better just imagining this table, then that it fine too.

Once you have your props in order, proceed to follow these steps:

1. Create two columns. On the left side, list down all the unfulfilled childhood needs that your parents could have fulfilled when you were a kid.

2. On the right side, write down the characteristics you think your parents should have had to fulfill those needs.

3. Think of who the ideal parents are and the characteristics that make them so good. Create a mental model of who these may be using all representational systems you might deem suitable. Make sure you paint the best picture of the perfect parents in your opinion and make sure you don't leave anything out. It might be something fairly simple, like them being supportive and helping you out with your homework, or it might be something more complex. This is *your* image of the perfect parents.

4. Think of these parents and imagine them in a situation where they would solve a problem to help you out. It might be something related to your behavior or it might be something related to the negative behavior of your peers in school. How are these parents taking action?

5. Jump back in time to the day you were born and imagine these ideal parents there, with you. Take a walk through your life so far and imagine your parents being there for you, supporting you, being calm and helping you out of challenging

situations as a kid. You can overlap this with actual situations you have experienced or create imaginary situations that are close to something you might have experienced.

6. Remedy your childhood wounds according to the aforementioned images and scenarios. Take your most poignant negative experiences and overlap them with the positive scenarios you have just created. Watch how your parents are now dealing with the situations that hurt you before.

7. Allow the feeling of warmth and protection to embrace you and take that feeling into your daily life. Take the positive emotions and allow them to flood your day-to-day life, to repair the negativity you have been experiencing in relation to your childhood memories. Accept the unconditional love.

8. Integrate the same feeling into your daily life and work with it as you would with an anchor (as described in the beginning of this chapter). If you feel overwhelmed with bad childhood memories or if you just feel that the negativity they built in you is resurfacing, go back to this anchor of peace and love you have created in your mind.

9. Observe your behavior. Is the exercise having any effect on it? How do you communicate with those around you (on a personal and professional level)

now? Have you managed to move (at least a little bit) out of your area of negativity?

These exercises are, of course, not *everything* there is to self-nurturing. They are just the tip of the iceberg, if we have to be honest. However, we believe that these particular practices have been found to be useful in the treatment of self-criticism and negativity. Therefore, we strongly recommend you to try them.

In addition to these specific exercises, we also recommend you to look into Hygge. You may have heard about it, as it has been a concept trending on social media (including Instagram). But take the time to actually go more in-depth with it and research about everything it means; it will most definitely help you build a life of self-nurturing.

In brief terms, "hygge" is a state of comfort, contempt, and coziness, as it is defined by the Danish. The concept goes far beyond words, though. Those who live for the "hygge" surround their entire lives with self-love. Their houses are made to be comfortable and decorated in a way that gets them closer to Mother Nature. Their spare time is spent doing things that bring them comfort and a sense of wellness—like reading by the fireplace, spending time with their loved ones, hiking in nature, and so on.

We encourage you to adopt a hygge lifestyle too. No matter how stressed your life may get, there is always room to take a few minutes and unwind. Yes, you may have a ton of reports to turn in on Monday, but you should still have time for yourself. Because how else will you ever be able to build a proper communication and relationship with yourself if you don't spend time doing things that you genuinely enjoy too?

We encourage everyone to practice self-nurturing. It is, without a doubt, one of the very best things you can do for yourself.

Strategy 9: Fractals

Fractals are one of the most complex NLP strategies. Initially brought into neuro-linguistic programming by Robert Dilts,[10] fractals are a concept that originated in geometry.

---

[10] Article of the Month Page. (2019). Retrieved 15 July 2019, from http://www.nlpu.com/Articles/artic24.htm

Basically, fractals are very complex geometric patterns that can be split into divisive parts that are, on their own, a smaller copy of the geometric pattern they were split from. They are called "self-similar" (because they are an approximate copy of the whole they came from) and scale-independent (because they look similar regardless of how you zoom in).

OK, but how are fractals related to NLP, you may ask?

Robert Dilts considered that fractals can show how simple processes that are born in the deep structures of our brain can create complex patterns at the surface of the structures. He designed two exercises to help NLP users improve their communication skills: the somatic fractal and the resource fractal, both of which we will discuss further on.

The Somatic Fractal

Using the Somatic Syntax theory, Robert Dilts designed an exercise meant to help people understand their deep intuition structures. The steps you need to take for this exercise are as follows:

1. This exercise should be done with a partner.

2. Think of a shape and ask your partner to close their eyes. The shape can be anything: a triangle, a square, anything you want, really.

3. Use your finger to "draw" the pattern of the shape in the air.

4. Gradually include other body parts in the movement to make it more complex.

5. Repeat this until as much of your body is involved in the movement. Keep in mind that the large movement you are at now should not necessarily imitate the smaller one you did at first. Try to see the small movement you did at first as the seed of this larger one (and make sure the gradual growth into the movement that includes the entire body is actually large).

6. Ask your partner to open their eyes and guess the original shape you were "drawing" at first based on what they are seeing now. The original shape is the "deep structure pattern," while the shape you are at now is the "somatic fractal."

   To seek the deep structure pattern, your partner will have to use their intuition to "narrow down" the pattern they see now to what could have been the pattern that generated it. Watch closely as they try to detect the deep structure pattern and how intuition plays a role in all of this.

7. Switch roles and practice the exercise again.

8. Observe your behavior in the following days and see if you can access the same kind of intuition when it comes to daily decisions and communications as well. You might not be able to do it after your first round of exercise, but you should observe your behavior at least to see how you progressed and if you can now communicate better as a result of your deeper understanding of how your own intuition works.

The Resource Fractal

The resource fractal focuses a lot on problem solving and creativity, but it can expand on how you live life to the fullest as well. What this fractal-based exercise plays on is your ability to create multi-representational systems, expressing the best state you can get in. To practice this, follow these steps:

1. Access your resourceful state, as it was described earlier in this book.

2. Create a movement pattern that expresses this resourceful state. This can be a free-form dance, for example. Allow yourself to do things your own way and allow yourself to be free of any kind of internal or external judgment. Move freely and create a pattern that simply expresses the state you are in.

3. Start adding variation to the movements. Do this subtly; don't change the pattern all of the sudden. Observe how it affects your state and how it connects to the deeper structure (the initial movement).

4. Transfer the movement to a different part of the body, following the same pattern. For instance, if you used your left hand to create this pattern, move up to the elbows, shoulders, neck, etc. Again, do this gently.

5. Transfer the movement to more parts of your body. Maybe even allow your entire body to perform the same patterned movement—your hands, your arms, your legs, your torso, even your facial expression.

6. Move the pattern into another representational system. Until now, you used the kinaesthetic senses to create the movement. Try moving into the visual realm by creating a walk through your

memories that expresses the resourceful state you are in. Or, why not, try to move it into the auditory realm by singing and creating sounds that express this state? If you want to, you can actually add words and describe soundscapes. Don't limit your creativity—do whatever it takes to express the wonderful state of resourcefulness you have accessed.

7. Once out of the exercise, observe your behavior and see if your creativity (in the kinaesthetic, auditory, and/or visual representational systems) is more enhanced. Notice if you can solve problems easier and with more creative solutions. Notice if you can simply experience the world better. Again, keep in mind that you might not be seeing tremendous changes from the first round of exercise, but the more you practice, the more you will advance.

The fractal exercises may sound a bit odd if you have never practiced anything like this before. However, if you practice continuously, you will definitely start seeing the benefits!

Strategy 10: Satir Categories

Virginia Satir is one of the first names associated with neuro-linguistic programming. A trained therapist, she was modeled according to the NLP concepts and, in turn, her own work became fundamental to neuro-linguistic programming. Her clinical studies gave birth to a whole new NLP modeling process called, perhaps not surprisingly, *The Virginia Satir Change Process Model.* Although not initially created for this purpose, her model has been applied to organizational change as well.

According to Satir's finding, people fall into five main categories. Each of these categories comes with its own body language, with its own communication patterns, and with its own attitudes.

Let's take a closer look at each of these categories, as per Virginia Satir's findings.

1. The Blamer

As the name suggests, the Blamer will always place the blame not on themselves, of course, but on someone else. They always externalize the blame by associating it with judgments that are, most of the time, based on severe distortions of the reality the Blamer perceives.

Additionally, the Blamers will always push their thoughts and emotions outward toward everyone else. As you may expect, more often than not, these emotions are quite toxic, which is also why Blamers are sometimes called "skunks."

One of the recurring body language signs of a Blamer is the pointed finger. When they point their finger, you know they are *blaming* someone. They also control their body language quite well and are frequently seen using a variety of tactics that support their blame. Very often, the blame they place on others sticks precisely because of these tactics and the way the Blamers don't leave much room for interpretation. The main reason their strategies work so well is because they don't over-generalize, and they don't blame without bringing any kind of proof (or at least not on the surface). They are quite ambiguous in their blaming, though; they use very fancy comparisons, and they usually make general statements, but their evidence is almost always thin, to say the least.

Sadly, Blamers are quite alienated from the rest of the people, precisely because their behavior pushes everyone away. They do tend to get along with people who are at least somewhat like-minded, and they usually tend to place the blame on those pertaining to other groups.

Despite the fact that they look quite confident, deep inside, Blamers are quite frail. In fact, their behavior is frequently born out of their own vulnerabilities. They fear judgment, they feel small, and they need to place the blame on everyone else because they want to be part of the "elite" group. In fact, the blaming they do is almost always in the name of something or someone bigger than them. It might be a religious institution, it might be the management team, it might be something political—but it almost always is something the Blamer aspires to in one way or another.

2. The Placater

Same as the Blamer, the Placater will be frequently noticed in situations where they place all the negativity as being someone else's fault. Since this type of personality is usually very concerned with their image (both physical and otherwise), they tend to be more diplomatic than the Blamer. When the fire ball is in their court, the Placater will throw it into someone else's courtyard. The Blamer, on the other hand, will throw it back (and perhaps add a bit of extra on top).

Most often, the Placater will be seen with their palms facing up. Their body position tends to be slouched too. Moreover, unlike the Blamer, they will be frequently seen violating the meta-model through cause and effect distortions, misuse of modal operators, and ambiguous verbs.

Placaters tend to also attract sympathy and empathy by using an attitude of self-complaint and self-pity. When it comes to facing the conflict, however, the Placater will simply disappear—they will either physically disappear or they will not engage in the conflict altogether, even if they are physically present.

3. The Computer

If there is someone who seems to be completely unemotional, it is this person. It's not that they don't *feel*—it's just that they cover up their feelings quite well (most often by simply using too many words).

The Computer will frequently come across as academic or scientific, but that is not always the case (not because they don't have the intelligence, but simply because their language is a mirroring of the kind of person they *want* to be, rather than the person they are).

When faced with someone else's emotions, the Computer will pull out the cool mask. They will act calm and collected, as if to counter-balance the emotions in the room (because there can never be anything too sentimental happening around them). Very frequently, they will dismiss and invalidate other people's emotions not necessarily because they don't care enough, but because they cannot work with their own feelings either. *Feelings*, in general, are a mathematical unknown to the Computer.

The Computer is frequently compared to Star Trek's Spock, precisely because they seem to come from a planet where everything has to be logical. Even their posture will resemble that of Spock: They will commonly be seen folding their arms (especially when they have to shield themselves from all the emotions flying around them). Sometimes, they take a neutral posture, and other times they might look a bit awkward. Their gestures are sometimes like those of the typical movie nerd: It seems that they are a bit disconnected from the actual person, a bit odd, and lacking a bit in consciousness.

Computer personalities are commonly associated with diagnoses on the autism spectrum (such as Asperger's syndrome), and this connects quite tightly with their inability to perceive and understand emotions at their face value.

In language, computers might sometimes use generalizations and they might sometimes omit using references, which, again, connects quite tightly to their inclination toward an academic stance in everything they say and do.

4. The Distracter

The Distracter is somewhat of a mix between all the typologies explained up to this point. Beyond the various characteristics they borrow from the Blamers, the Computers, and the Placaters, Distracters have a very poignant characteristic that is all their own: They manipulate. And they don't manipulate in just any way; they do it by distracting their communication partner. They can be compared to a stoat (a type of weasel) that does an elaborate dance to distract its victim before attacking. Distracters may not get physically aggressive, but they usually confuse their interlocutor or they simply drain their energy to bring communication into their winning field.

Having a proper conversation with the Distracter is almost impossible—and this is part of their strategy, actually. They are almost never held accountable for their actions, precisely because actual communication doesn't happen to them, so holding them accountable for anything is nearly impossible too.

Distracters are not always fully conscious of their actions and communication style. They can bring someone to exasperation precisely because they gesticulate a lot when communicating, but they don't actually *say* much. At a subconscious level, they intuitively know just how to escalate their distraction as needed, just enough to confuse the person(s) in front of them by using too many stimuli. They also tend to generalize a lot, they switch topics a lot, and they very frequently omit references, as well.

5. The Leveler

As the name suggests, this typology is the one who will always try to level things down, and their body language is quite revealing in this sense too. They are frequently seen with their palms facing downwards, as if they are telling everyone to relax and think things through.

They almost never dramatize a situation, so even if they have to blame something on someone else, they do it objectively and fairly. They do tend to upset other people, but that is mostly because they are very much in touch with reality and because they know their interests. Moreover, they tend to dismiss manipulation (including the manipulative styles of the other typologies described here).

Levelers are almost always great mediators, and that is because they have the ability to see both sides of an argument and objectively weigh in on the situation, not allowing their own bias to take over.

According to Virginia Satir, nobody should be fixed into *one* style only. People should be flexible so that they can adapt to multiple types of situations and bring forward solutions for multiple types of problems.

That includes the Leveler as well. On the surface, they sound like the ideal style, but in fact, they can be troublesome (for themselves, if not for anyone else) if they are stuck in the same typology all the time. When mediating, the Leveler needs to know how to adapt to different styles according to the prerequisites of the situation and its complexities.

The same goal of flexibility should be applied to all typologies. There is no "right" or "wrong" typology in NLP (because, remember, as it was also mentioned before, everyone's purposes are inherently positive).

So, how do you build rapport with these people? Here are some tips:

- Don't put a Blamer in defensive mode. Pace them without making them feel that they should defend themselves and their vulnerability. For instance, you could act like you are upset for the same reason as the Blamer is. Once rapport has been established, the Blamer will find it much easier to connect with you and you might actually win their trust too—especially since not many people even attempt to try to do that.

- Creating rapport with the Placater can be quite easy, and this is mostly related to the fact that they need attention and understanding more than anything. The secret lies in how you keep them in touch with their own responsibilities.

- When it comes to Distracters, you should know that they tend to be quite open to proper communication and even rapport. Although they hide behind a lot of gestures and confusing strategies, they don't necessarily want to put people away. The key lies in not confronting them directly and being as non-threatening as you can.

  If they are trying to distract you from something, don't bring it back and point it out to them. Stay firm when it comes to facts and data, and make sure your position is quite clear to them. Then, allow the Distracter to take you on their typical detour so that they don't feel threatened. Do drop hints about the fact that they have to do what has to be done, but don't be too aggressive with it. This will bring the Distracter back to your own agenda every time they try to take off to the lands of confusion. This will eventually exhaust the Distracter's energy, and they will give in to your way.

- Levelers are quite easy to deal with since, as an NLP practitioner, you see things mostly the same way as they do. If you have to disagree with them, make sure you are coherent and that you have your facts in your back pocket because the Leveler will definitely respect that.

When dealing with the various categories described by Virginia Satir, it is essential that you do not assume that you will be dealing with the worst of the worst. Even if you see someone when they are at their most manipulative, for example, don't assume they will always be like that. Even if it's unconsciously, most people show some degree of flexibility, and they do not always behave irrationally.

Take a Leveler stance every time you have to interact with someone who is more difficult or displays more poignant characteristics from one category or another. Be balanced—that is the best position to start any kind of interaction from.

We genuinely hope the strategies described in this chapter have helped you go more in-depth with the various applications of NLP and how they can actually help you create better relationships both with people you've known for decades as well as people you have just met.

More than anything, though, we hope these strategies will help you bring more balance into your life because the best way to start a race is not by being strained, but in a state of pure equilibrium.

The very last chapter of this book is dedicated to helping you apply neuro-linguistic programming in your own life. Take it as a brief review of everything you have learned thus far—a way to allow all the information to cement and work its way into your daily habits, actions, and communications.

CHAPTER 9:
INTEGRATING NLP IN YOUR LIFE

Neuro-linguistic programming can be a genuine life-changing experience. It can change you inside and out. It can change the way you interact with everyone around you, from your parents and your loved ones to the C-level people you might meet in various companies.

Like most real changes, though, you shouldn't expect it to happen overnight. You wouldn't expect to lose 20 pounds or gain 10 pounds of muscle overnight. You wouldn't expect a successful career in anything to happen overnight. And you wouldn't expect all the negativity you have been experiencing in your life to simply vanish after a good night's sleep.

So, you shouldn't expect neuro-linguistic programming to work its benefits into your life overnight as well. Truth be told, it's an ever-growing process, one that will make you better at everything you endeavor to do. But you should take it slowly.

To help you successfully integrate NLP in your life, we have collected some of the essential tips you should definitely include in your strategy of adopting neuro-linguistic programming.

Start Small

We know that everything we have described here sounds amazing and that you can't wait to try it *all* and see how it plays out in your life. However, our recommendation is that you start small on everything. First and foremost, give yourself time to internalize all the information. While far from being a complete look at NLP (it would take entire libraries for that), the book at hand was, we hope, quite rich in information. So it is completely natural that you might want to come back to it, partially or not.

Take your time. Read and re-read. Allow all of this to settle in. And then, start to slowly bring all the advice we have given you into your life. Start with a small conversation with a coworker, for example. Notice how they use language, notice how their body emits messages too. See if you can mirror that, for example, and observe the results.

Gradually work your way up to applying neuro-linguistic programming techniques once a day, every day, for a given amount of time. See how it works, observe what functions and what doesn't and when. Take it slowly; you really don't have to rush with this!

Take each piece of information and each strategy we have described here one by one and perfect them. Neuro-linguistic programming takes hard work the same way a very muscular body requires hard work. In fact, you can actually look at how your brain functions and train it with NLP strategies the same way you would with any other muscle in your body: by starting slowly and working your way up.

Accept That It May Not Always Work

Don't get us wrong here: We are very strong proponents of neuro-linguistic programming and everything it does. But, especially at first, you might find yourself in situations where your techniques don't work (or, at least, don't work entirely).

That is OK. Every attempt that doesn't work (and no, we won't call it *a failure* because that concept simply does not exist in NLP) is a step forward, even if it might not look like it now. Yet, every time you try and don't necessarily succeed in achieving your goal, you learn something. It may be something about the way you use your language. It may be about your interlocutor's language. Or it may simply be something that needs some finessing.

Try again. Work your way toward your expected goal one step at a time applying NLP with care and attention to detail.

Don't Self-Criticize

To be completely honest, self-criticism is the death of all evolution. Do you think the first man who learned how to make fire achieved his goal the very first time he tried it? Probably not. And do you think he drowned in a puddle of self-criticism and self-pity? Probably not.

If something doesn't work, observe the details and see how you can make it work, but don't criticize yourself for it. Self-compassion is essential to achieving the NLP goals, it is essential when you want to be happy, and, ultimately, it is essential for those of you who want to achieve a fearless, thriving, and victorious life.

Accept That Some People May Not Like It

Ideally, you want to make sure your NLP strategies are not obvious. For instance, when you try to mirror someone, you want to be as subtle as you possibly can.

The thing is that some people may actually *sniff* it out. Instinctually or not (because they may have read about it too), some people may perceive your attempt to create rapport with them as a way by which you are trying to manipulate them. We all know NLP is as far from that as possible. But some people may not like it when it is done *on them.*

Accept that and move on. You simply cannot be everything for everyone, and that is OK too.

Enjoy Your Successes

NLP may not work all the time, but when it does, it can give you a special kind of satisfaction. It's not the satisfaction of winning the lottery or getting a raise. It's the satisfaction of an athlete who has finally managed to push their boundaries beyond what everyone else expected of them.

This doesn't mean you should gloat about your success. It means you can give yourself a pat on the back. You can give yourself an internal smile. You can give yourself congratulations for having managed to control your language and your meta-programs to win a communication over to your side.

Most importantly, though, take your lesson of success and bring it forward. See what could be better. See what other types of situations you could apply the same technique for.

Integrating NLP in your life may be the very best thing you will ever do for yourself. Take it slowly, be patient, be diligent, and believe in yourself; thousands and thousands have already changed their lives as a result of applying neuro-linguistic programming techniques in their lives. And you can very soon become one of them too!

CONCLUSION

We hope this book has been useful to you. Regardless of who you are and what your life goals are, you deserve to be happy.

Happiness cannot be a one-size-fits-all recipe. It's just not how it works. Many will try to advertise that happiness lies in expensive clothes or luxurious vacations. Others will try to tell you that it's all about weight loss and the perfect body. And others will aim lower, telling you that happiness is in a particular brand of lipstick or after-shave, a chocolate bar, or a specific restaurant.

In reality, happiness is the sum of the things that make *you* feel contempt. Believe it or not, you don't need the expensive clothes, the luxurious vacations, or even that lipstick or after-shave to be happy. You might want them, and they might contribute to your overall feeling of contentment. But you don't *need* them.

And if you do find that you *need* them, it's not those specific things you should be after. It should probably be something on a higher level, like, for example, your ability to earn an above-average living, your ability to monetize your skills and talents, your ability to create networks of people that will ensure a smooth flow for your business, and so on.

Neuro-linguistic programming promises happiness that transcends all those specifics. When you learn how to communicate, you can literally rule the world. There's no evil laughter in the background, though; it's a completely different kind of "ruling of the world."

It's the kind that allows you to rule, first and foremost, over your own kingdom of thoughts. It allows you to take control over who you are and who you project yourself to be out in the world. It allows you to be more in tune with yourself and more in tune with everyone else around you.

Over the course of history, words have taken over worlds more than once. Sadly, most of the time, it was the evil-doers that had the best words. We won't get into a political debate here, nor do we want to bum you out. But, for a brief second in time and space, imagine all the power of the 20th-century rulers unleashed toward the betterment of mankind.

And imagine that you can be part of the machinery that sets that in action. You can actually be the change you want to see in the world. You can actually be a person who understands people, who can empathize with them, who can manipulate them not in the negative sense, but in the sense of helping them find their own path.

That is what neuro-linguistic programming is all about. Perhaps not a coincidence, NLP was born in the wake of the post-WWII world, a world that had been torn apart by men who knew the power of words and what they can do when masses are wielded in one direction or another.

The way you use your language matters, precisely because language is the very essence of what you are as a human being. Unlike computers, you don't see zeros and ones. You always think in *words*. Every image you have in your head has a very tightly correlated set of sounds or, in some cases, a set of linguistic symbols you associate with it. That is how we are wired, and when you learn how to truly wire and unwire the patterns your brain has created all on its own, you can take control.

You can take control of your life. Of your own self. Of your negative emotions. Of every single small action that you may have been doing unconsciously. Of everything you want to achieve in your life.

We don't want to promise you the moon and then not deliver. We want you to experience the altitude of change NLP can bring into your life *on your own skin*. Hopefully, this book has given you the tools to create the NLP mind map you want in your life and the tools to help you create bridges of communication that will eventually get you every single thing you want.

NLP lingers at the border between science and art. It plays with language, but it taps into deeply scientific prerequisites. It uses strategy, but it calls for action that comes from the heart before anything. It paints the world map of your own brain, but it does so using data-driven color picking.

Take it, embrace it, work it into your life, and create the future you deserve. There's so much waiting for you beyond the horizon; you just have to dare to reach out and create the bridge that will take you there!

References

[Infographic] - 6 Statistics On Networking And Steps For Future Success | Ryze. (2019). Retrieved 22 July 2019, from https://ryzeapp.co/infographic-six-statistics-on-networking/

Article of the Month Page. (2019). Retrieved 15 July 2019, from http://www.nlpu.com/Articles/artic24.htm

Ashok, S., & Santhakumar, A. (2002). NLP to promote TQM for effective implementation of ISO 9000. Managerial Auditing Journal, 5(17), 261-265.

Definition of COMMUNICATION. (2019). Retrieved 22 July 2019, from https://www.merriam-webster.com/dictionary/communication

Infographic: the importance of face to face networking. (2019). Retrieved 22 July 2019, from https://www.virgin.com/entrepreneur/infographic-the-importance-of-face-to-face-networking

Information Processing Theory (G. Miller) - InstructionalDesign.org. (2019). Retrieved 22 July 2019, from https://www.instructionaldesign.org/theories/information-processing/

Larousse, É. (2019). Définitions: rapporter - Dictionnaire de français Larousse. Retrieved 22 July 2019, from https://www.larousse.fr/dictionnaires/francais/rapporter/66519?q=rapporter#65769

NLP Case Studies - How Could NLP Help Me? - NLP - Neuro-Linguistic Programming. (2019). Retrieved 22 July 2019, from https://anlp.org/how-could-nlp-help-me.php

RAPPORT | meaning in the Cambridge English Dictionary. (2019). Retrieved 22 July 2019, from https://dictionary.cambridge.org/dictionary/english/rapport?q=rapport+

Socrates: Know Yourself. (2019). Retrieved 22 July 2019, from https://www.the-philosophy.com/socrates-know-yourself

Printed in Great Britain
by Amazon